How to Play Pickleball for Beginners

Mastering Rules, Racket Techniques, Court Etiquette, Scoring Strategies, and Expert Tips for Singles and Doubles

Table of Contents

Introduction 1

Chapter 1: Understanding the Game of Pickleball 3

Chapter 2: Getting Started with Pickleball 10

Chapter 3: Mastering the Rules of Pickleball................ 27

Chapter 4: Learning Racquet Techniques 41

Chapter 5: Navigating the Pickleball Court.................. 58

Chapter 6: Court Etiquette and Sportsmanship 64

Chapter 7: Scoring Strategies 74

Chapter 8: Mastering Singles and Thriving in
Doubles Play 85

Chapter 9: Common Mistakes and How to
Avoid Them... 94

Chapter 10: Tips from Pickleball Experts 105

Chapter 11: Staying Safe and Injury-Free 119

Chapter 12: Getting Involved in the Pickleball
Community 127

Bonus Chapter: Fun Pickleball Facts......................... 131

Conclusion 139

References 141

Introduction

Pickleball is a word being bandied around more and more these days, and it has absolutely nothing to do with fermented cucumbers! Pickleball is simply a ball and racquet game, albeit one of the most popular and fastest-growing, at least in America. It started as a game designed to amuse children but is now a pro sport with many competitive players. That doesn't mean only pros can play it, though. Millions of people still play it for fun as a family or community game, and there's no need for everyone to be at peak fitness, nor do they need to be young. After all, the game was once one of the most popular games for seniors!

You will find this guide different from all the others. It is down to earth, written in plain language, and explains everything you need to know about Pickleball. It will tell you where the game started, the rules, the equipment you need, and many strategies to help you learn and win every match you play. It is a well-illustrated guide that shows and tells you what you need to know, and you'll find it easy to follow.

With millions of players, Pickleball is now one of the best-known sports, but it's also a fun, social game you can play with friends. With one of the largest communities of all sports, it's a place where you can meet others, make new friends, and improve your life.

So, what are you waiting for? Let's learn about Pickleball and how to start playing it right away.

Chapter 1: Understanding the Game of Pickleball

Pickleball is a simple racquet sport, a combination of certain elements from table tennis, tennis, and badminton, played on a court. The racquet is a hard paddle, and the sport is played with a plastic ball full of holes – you'll learn more about these in a later chapter.

1.   Pickleball is a sport combining elements of tennis, table tennis, and badminton. Source: https://unsplash.com/photos/a-tennis-racket-and-three-balls-on-a-tennis-court-om-cfOuEHOw?utm_source=unsplash&utm_medium=referral&utm_content=creditShareLink

It can be a doubles competition with two players from two teams or a singles match with two players. It really is quite a simple game; all you need to do is knock the ball from one side of the court to the other. Of course, there is a little more to it than that. Players can score points in certain circumstances, usually if their opponent doesn't knock the ball back or they hit it out of bounds.

Pickleball is one of the easiest sports to learn, with no limits or rules on age, fitness, or skill. While it is incredibly popular in the USA, it is also beginning to spread worldwide.

How It Compares to Other Sports

When you watch a Pickleball game, you may think it is similar to squash, tennis, badminton, and other racquet sports. It involves using a racquet to hit a small ball over a net between players. In Pickleball, the racquet is a small, hard one shaped like a paddle, and it is used to hit a small plastic ball perforated with holes.

However, there are more similarities as Pickleball shares the same court style and rules as some other racquet sports.

Another huge similarity lies in Pickleball being a team sport. However, despite being a team sport mostly played in doubles, it can be played as a singles game between two opponents. However, regardless of whether you play singles or doubles, you play as a team, and the premise remains the same – score points to win the game. This is common in most similar sports, as players must work together to win the game.

Another similarity is the physical side of the game. Pickleball is a great way to improve your fitness levels. It is a physical game, as you are constantly on the move; your whole body moves as you run to reach the ball and hit it back to your opponents. You do need to be somewhat fit to play it, but the more you play, the fitter you will get and the more stamina you will have.

That said, there are a few differences. The primary difference is the court size and equipment. Everything about Pickleball is smaller than the other racquet sports, including the courts, balls, and racquets. This makes Pickleball a fast game needing precise shots and fast reflexes.

The point system is another variation. In this game, the player can only get points when the serving team serves a fault, or the receiving team returns the ball out of bounds. In contrast, points can be scored in many ways in other racquet sports. Pickleball's unique system means the players must play their game strategically, planning their shots and working out what their opponents will do.

Pickleball's Origins

The first game of Pickleball was played in 1965, and it took place on Bainbridge Island in Washington. Barney McCallum, Joel Pritchard, and Bill Bell, who were very close, created the game while looking for a fun activity to do during the summer. They combined components from badminton, tennis, and table tennis to create the game we know today. To begin with, they used a Wiffle ball to play with, using badminton paddles on a temporary court they drew out on a badminton court. Before long, they realized that their game could be a big thing, and they started to spread the news to their friends and families.

The game soon became popular on Bainbridge Island, and the three men soon began to draw up an official set of rules. It didn't take them long either to start making their own

Pickleball sets and selling them, including the paddles and balls.

Pickleball started to spread across Washington. In the early part of the 1970s, it also began spreading to other areas in the States, with YMCAs and schools adopting Pickleball. It wasn't long before it was a popular inclusion in recreation and physical education programs. Now, it is played everywhere in the world.

The Pickleball Association, Tournaments, and Senior Games

The first tournament was played in Seattle in 1976, and, with its popularity growing, there are now a large number of annual tournaments across the country. The most popular has to be the USA Open Pickleball Championship.

The USAPA (United States of America Pickleball Association) was founded in 1984. Originally started to promote Pickleball, the Association is now responsible for setting the official rules, ensuring players comply with them, and setting up official tournaments.

In 2016, the PPA (Professional Pickleball Association) was formed, ensuring the sport was promoted professionally. They ensure professional tournaments are organized and act as a governing body for pro players.

Now, Pickleball is part of the Senior Games, an event similar to the Olympics for older athletes. In 2010, the first Senior Games was played and are now played biannually.

Popularity Growth and Professional Players

Although it started life as a small family sport, Pickleball has grown to be incredibly popular; as each year passes, more players join, and more courts and clubs are set up. It can now be considered one of America's most popular and fastest-growing sports.

Over time, the game's popularity led to a significant increase in Pickleball courts and facilities. Courts are now included in many schools, parks, and recreation centers, and you can also find a large number of facilities purely for the game.

Of course, as its popularity grew, more people wanted to become professional players. Pro players compete in PPA-organized tournaments and can earn money when they compete and win. Some players are so successful that they have made Pickleball their sole income-earning career.

This has provided the sport with a positive image. While it is still played as a fun game by many, professional players compete for glory and money – not only do they compete in tournaments to earn money, but they also teach the sport at clubs and schools.

Pickleball's Impact and Its Future

It's undeniable that Pickleball has significantly impacted the world of sport. It has introduced so many people to the excitement racquet sports bring and has helped many to get fit and keep active, especially older people. It's also a great way for communities and families to bond.

The future of this game is looking very bright indeed, and as each year passes, it won't get any less popular. It is easy to learn, and your age doesn't matter; you can play it, if only for fun.

Here's some information about Pickleball:

- While almost five million people play in the USA alone, tournaments are now held in countries across the world.

- While Pickleball has been a game for seniors for a long time, it is now played by all ages, from 4 to 94.

- There's no need for expensive equipment, not to start with. You can play in a small space, and you only need a net, a pair of racquets, and plastic balls.

It is a fast game, and if you are to learn to play it right, you must have the proper equipment.

Why Pickleball Is a Great Sport

Typically played with 2 or 4 players on a small court, Pickleball is a racquet sport that offers players plenty of benefits, not least being great for health and socialization. Single games not played as part of a tournament can last just 15 minutes, and you can start playing by finding your nearest Pickleball court or facility.

The Health Benefits

Everyone can benefit from keeping active and working out; Pickleball offers exercise for the body, mind, and soul. The mental health benefits include:

- Relieves anxiety.

- Reduction in depression symptoms.

- Relieves tension.

- Enables better relaxation and sleep.

If you suffer from loneliness and seasonal depression, going out and meeting people can help combat symptoms. A study on middle-aged and older adults who played Pickleball several times weekly showed improvements in cardio fitness and blood pressure.

Socialization

Where sports and activities like cycling and running can be quite lonely, Pickleball is more social. Several players are needed, and fans and players typically meet up regularly. Because the game attracts a wide range of demographics, people are constantly joining, from youngsters with plenty of energy to burn off to older people who want to meet new people.

Pickleball is also well-suited to leagues, encouraging large groups of people to come together to play. This game is social, and it encourages interaction between players of all ages.

Affordable

With most sports, the more involved you get, the more expensive it gets, especially when buying new clothes, equipment, and specialized gear. Pickleball is the exception to that. Most municipal courts are free to use, league play costs far less than many other racquet sports, and the equipment is cheap, too. You don't even need a court if you are only playing for fun. Simply mark your own out on the ground!

Quick and Fun

Lastly, if you are looking for a way to fill in a short period during your busy day, Pickleball is for you. People these days lead busy lives, but you can fit in a single Pickleball match in just 15 minutes. It's a lot of fun to play, a great way to keep fit, and there are no limits on how long you can or should play.

Chapter 2: Getting Started with Pickleball

If you are ready to dive into what Pickleball is all about, it's time to get started. We'll begin with the equipment you need.

Pickleball Equipment

Like any sport, you need certain equipment to play Pickleball, mainly racquets, balls, net, and posts. However, you should consider some other things, including shoes, clothes, glasses, and gloves. These will all be discussed in this chapter.

First, why is the right equipment so important?

It's simple. Like any sport, your equipment will impact your performance and effectiveness during gameplay. That means purchasing equipment that suits your height, age, gender, weight, and skill level. Using the right equipment will minimize the risks of falling or hurting yourself when the game gets intense. The right shoes are also important, as the last thing you need is sore or injured feet. Pickleball is a fast-moving game; you'll be running and jumping about a hard court. The biggest tip here is not to play in sandals, flip-flops, or bare-footed, even if that's how you normally spend your day.

We'll start with the most important piece of equipment.

Pickleball Racquet

2.   Carbon fiber Pickleball racquet. Source: https://unsplash.com/photos/a-person-holding-a-tennis-racquet-on-top-of-a-tennis-court-ECAxgPmccLA?utm_source=unsplash&utm_medium=referral&utm_content=creditShareLink

Every Pickleball racquet is different, which is why it is so important to choose the right one. That means you need to think about a few things; five things to be precise:

Core Materials

This is the one thing that seems to be forgotten about, especially by beginners, likely because you don't see it. The core makes up the guts of the racquet, usually made of a honeycomb of shapes between the racquet faces. This core may be made of several different materials in multiple structures and techniques.

While core materials may be any of a number of options, Nomex and polymer are the two main ones:

- **Nomex**: This material is used for power. It is a dense, strong, light polyamide typically used in airplane floors, military uniforms, and many other places where strong, light material is required. It is also flame-resistant. It is generally made into much smaller honeycombs than other materials, which means there are more of them, increasing the core's surface area and creating rigidity, which leads to power.

- **Polymer**: This material also produces power, but it also aids control. It is by far the most commonly used material and is often called a polypropylene core or polycore. It is more flexible and durable, providing control and power, and should be the first core material a beginner looks for.

The right material offers accuracy, power, and control while decreasing vibration and shock.

Core Thickness

Staying with the core, the material isn't the only important aspect. Its depth or thickness also plays an important role. The core thickness is the gap between each external edge – the depth of the core inside. This is typically measured in millimeters – thick cores are typically 16 mm or close to it, while thinner ones are nearer 11 mm. You may even come across the thickness measured in inches – ½-inch is roughly

13 mm, a medium core thickness. The thick and thin cores are approximately 1/16th inch thicker or thinner.

So, why is thickness important?

If your racquet has a thick core, it gives you better control when hitting the ball. This is because a thick core softens the ball's impact on the racquet. In contrast, a thinner core gives you more power. There is a fine line in getting this right when you choose a Pickleball racquet, but getting the right combination of core material and thickness will make all the difference in how you play.

Surface Material

Another area that surprises many players is how many variations in surface materials there are to choose from. The 3 most popular materials are fiberglass, carbon fiber, and graphite.

- **Fiberglass**: The heaviest material, yet it is the most flexible of all. When you hit a ball with a fiberglass racquet, the ball sinks into the surface a bit before firing off – think of it as a tight spring uncoiling. The elasticity and the extra weight provide a lot of power.

- **Graphite**: A lightweight material, graphite is also incredibly strong, making it the ideal material for a Pickleball racquet. When you hit a ball with a graphite racquet, its strength spreads the force across the whole racquet's face. While this gives your racquet a decent-sized sweet spot, it does lose you a certain amount of power.

- **Carbon Fiber**: This material is a subtype of graphite but is much stronger and lighter. It is incredibly popular on Pickleball racquets and offers a great balance of power and finesse – in one racquet, you get the best of what the fiberglass and graphite racquets offer.

As you've probably gathered, the surface material is important as it impacts power and control in every shot.

Grip Size

The next thing you need to consider is the grip size – it must fit your hands and be comfortable. This is not about the grip style but the grip dimensions.

You will often hear people talking about handles and grips as the same thing, which, in some circumstances, is okay. However, when you consider circumference and length, handles and grips are not the same. The handle length is the distance from the racquet neck to the jewel on the grip; the grip circumference is the distance around the handle.

When you go to buy a racquet, you will see these measurements listed in the specs. Grip size may be called circumference, and the handle length may be referred to as grip length, but you will typically see the measurements listed in inches.

There are several options for grip sizes, but most will typically be 3.875 inches to 4.375 inches – the sizes jump in increments of 1/16th inch. Most players go for 4 1/8th inch to 4 3/8th inch – the lower size can have tape added to increase it.

One of the biggest things to consider when looking at grip size is the core thickness – small grips are limited based on core thickness. The racquet's structural integrity may be compromised when you go over a certain threshold.

Seriously though, the only real way to work out the grip size that suits you is to pick up some racquets, play some games, and see what works and what doesn't. Consider this –

if you choose too small a grip, you will fumble your shots and suffer from a lack of control and fatigue. Too big, and your grip will never be right, leading to a lack of control. And that's without considering discomfort – there's no way you can play properly if you aren't comfortable!

Racquet Weight

Finally, you need to think about your racquet weight – an important consideration. Pickleball racquets are usually divided into three classes:

- **Midweight**: 7.3 ounces to 8.5 ounces
- **Lightweight**: 7.3 ounces or lower
- **Heavyweight**: 8.5 ounces or higher

Newbies are better off starting with a midweight racquet. The heavyweights give better power, and lightweight racquets allow you more control.

You should choose a lightweight racquet if you want great control and better reaction times. This is the best option for playing near the net when you want gentle dinks and aren't bothered about power. However, this does come with its downsides – the impact on your arm.

Lighter racquets don't absorb much energy with each hit, and your arm has to do the heavy work. Therefore, this isn't a great option if you have problems with your hitting arm, i.e., you've had golf or tennis elbow.

The midweights provide the right balance between control and power and are a great racquet for new players but suit all skill levels. Conversely, the heavyweight racquets offer significant power to every shot. However, these are not suited to beginners as your arm will tire very quickly – heavy racquets need more control and better placement, which beginners rarely have at the start. Heavyweight racquets are also not ideal if you already have an injury to your arm. That said, heavier racquets do provide better swing and motion.

The Balancing Act

It's clear to see that Pickleball racquets are all different; the one-size-fits-all solution definitely does not apply here. You need to consider all five of the above elements to get the right balance – while the surface material may give you power, your grip size could offer better control but less power.

Start with a baseline of skill level and preference – you should know what you like and then match that to your weaknesses and strengths on the Pickleball court. In that way, you'll get the right racquet for your needs.

Pickleball Balls

You may think all Pickleball balls are the same, but you would be wrong. First, they are classified into two groups – indoor and outdoor balls. But what's the difference between them?

3. Outdoor Pickleball balls. Source: E is for Ian, CC BY-SA 4.0 <https://creativecommons.org/licenses/by-sa/4.0>, via Wikimedia Commons: https://commons.wikimedia.org/wiki/File:Pickleball_balls.jpg

- **Holes**: Indoor balls have 40 holes close together, while outdoor balls only have 26 and are widely spaced. The reason concerns aerodynamics and reducing the risk of external factors, such as wind. Because outdoor balls have smaller holes, they are less affected by the wind.

- **Hole Diameter**: The holes on indoor balls are typically 0.43 inches in diameter, while those on outdoor balls are 0.282 inches. This means the holes on the indoor balls are roughly 40% larger than those on outdoor balls.

- **Weight**: For a variety of reasons, indoor balls are typically much lighter in weight than outdoor balls. Indoor balls feature fewer holes than outside balls but cover a bigger surface area. Indoor balls are lighter than outdoor balls since they don't have any negative space. Outdoor balls need to be heavier because they're more durable in different weather conditions. However, while outdoor balls are heavier, the difference is less than a percent. On average, an outdoor ball weighs 0.925 ounces, while an indoor ball weighs 0.855 ounces.

- **Hardness**: Pickleball balls are typically plastic, but not all plastics are the same. The durometer hardness test measures their hardness – the scale runs from 0 to 100, with 100 being the hardest. Outdoor balls are usually harder than their indoor counterparts, and this is down to the materials, thickness, and weight. Harder balls provide faster play, while softer balls are slower and better for indoor play.

- **Durability**: Pickleball balls do not last forever and, regardless of whether indoor or outdoor, will lose shape and go soft over time. Outdoor balls also tend to crack. The harder the material used to construct the ball, the shorter its lifespan will be. This means indoor balls have better durability because they are softer, and whereas outdoor balls crack, split, and go out of shape, indoor balls tend to go soft at the end of their lifespan.

Technically, you can use outdoor balls indoors and vice versa, but it's not advisable. If you use an indoor ball outside, it will play slowly, and be too soft to fight the wind. More commonly, outdoor balls are used indoors but, again, not very often. It's best to stick to using the right ball for where you are playing.

Pickleball Net

The Pickleball net is very important, but choosing the right one won't be easy, given the number of options. These are the two factors you need to consider:

- **Dimensions**: The official rules state that a net must be 34 inches tall in the center, 36 inches at the sides, 22 feet wide, and the posts 20 feet apart. There should also be a center strap to stop the net from sagging and hold it tight. Net height plays an important part in the ball's trajectory – the higher the net, the harder it is to lob the ball over it, while the net's width dictates the court size and player positioning.

- **Materials**: Nets can be constructed from polyester, nylon, or vinyl. Nylon is the most common because it is durable and light, while polyester suits those who need an easy-to-maintain net. Vinyl nets also offer durability but are more expensive. Higher-quality nets will typically last much longer and perform much better than lower-quality nets.

Some people choose to play with a tennis net but, while this is possible, it isn't recommended. These are usually higher, making it harder to play, and are typically wider, which affects gameplay and player positioning.

Some people play without a net, but this isn't ideal. The net helps set out the court boundaries, and not having one makes it difficult to tell if a ball has landed in or out of bounds.

Pickleball Clothing

Like all sports, you need the right clothing to play Pickleball for several reasons. Bear the following points in mind when you buy Pickleball clothing:

- **Comfort**: This is your main priority because Pickleball requires a significant amount of movement, and you must ensure your clothes aren't restrictive or uncomfortable. Choose clothes made of breathable, lightweight material.

- **Flexibility**: Because of the amount of movement, you need clothes that allow you to move. They should be stretchy and flexible for indoor play or tight but not restrictive if you play outdoors. Tight clothing can help you eliminate wind resistance and ensure better performance.

- **Durability**: Pickleball can sometimes be rough, so choose durable clothing that can stand up to wear and tear. Clothing should have reinforced seams and good zips, as these can help reduce the risk of tears and rips.

- **Moisture-Wicking**: Clothes made from this type of material keep sweat away from your body. This will cool you down and keep you dry while playing, and they dry quickly.

- **UV Protection**: Outdoor players should wear clothing with built-in UV protection, as this protects you from the sun's harmful rays. The best ones have a UPF rating of at least 50.

Whatever clothing you choose, comfort must always be your top priority.

Pickleball Gloves

Gloves are important as they protect your hands, reduce the risk of calluses and blisters, and eliminate hand injuries. They also help you grip the racquet better, allowing for more accuracy. Consider the following factors when you are purchasing Pickleball gloves:

- **Size**: Like any glove, a Pickleball glove will only help you if it fits properly. If your glove bunches around your palm, it will restrict your ability to hold your racquet. The right-fitting glove will feel like a second skin. Avoid one-size-fits-all gloves – these never fit anyone properly.

- **Palm Material**: This plays an important role in your gameplay. The most common materials are goatskin leather, Cabretta leather, tackified leather, and synthetic leather. Cabretta leather comes from hair-producing sheep and is tough but comfortable. Goatskin is also a good material but isn't quite so soft or durable as Cabretta, while tackified leather is usually used in football and riding gloves and can help with racquet grip. Lastly, synthetic leather is the cheapest and not as soft as real leather.

- **Adjustability**: While your gloves should feel like a second skin, you must still be able to adjust them. The most common method is via Velcro straps with a slant that follows the wrist.

- **Breathability**: Some gloves have mesh or small holes for ventilation, which helps stop your hands from sweating. Gloves made of Spandex, Lycra, and Neoprene can offer you great cushioning, airflow, and absorption.

- **Moisture Control**: You want gloves that absorb or wick moisture away from your hands, enabling a better grip on your racquet.

- **Durability**: Quality is important. You don't want gloves that fall apart at the slightest use. Buy the right gloves now, and you won't be running to the store every week to replace them!

And if you are fashion-conscious, make sure you choose a pair that looks stylish while incorporating all of the above.

Pickleball Glasses

4. *Pickleball glasses. Source: https://www.pxfuel.com/en/free-photo-jlxpb*

You may want to wear Pickleball glasses for several reasons, primarily because you need them to see accurately. However, they must not be made of glass, as this can shatter easily.

If you opt to wear glasses, avoid buying glass lenses; choose plastic instead. This is because glasses can break and cause injury to the player, while plastic models are less likely to crack or shatter in case of an accident. You also need to consider the lens shape, which typically comes in two styles:

- **Round**: Designed for close vision, these help you find your ball and offer great peripheral vision.

- **Fitted Lids**: These may be rectangular or square, and what you choose is down to your preferences. These do not have any openings and are often called lensless glasses.

Remember the following when buying glasses:

- **Impact Resistant**: The material should be strong and shatter-proof. You are bound to get hit once or twice and don't want your glasses breaking. If you can, get polycarbonate.

- **UV Protection**: Protects your eyes from the sun, especially if you are playing outdoors.

- **Good Fit**: Your glasses should be secure and snug, ensuring they cannot fall off. Try to get glasses with a slip-resistant frame or adjustable nose pads.

- **Vision**: Make sure your glasses have a lens tint that gives you better vision. For example, brown tints provide better color contrast, yellow or gray provide contrast and reduce glare, while a rose tint makes details sharper.

It should be obvious why you should wear glasses when playing Pickleball. They keep the sweat, dirt, and sun out of your eyes, enabling better vision all around.

Pickleball Shoes

The right shoes are as important when playing Pickleball as with any other sport. But you shouldn't wear just any old shoes as there are several things you need to consider:

- **Traction**: Choose shoes with a herringbone or diamond pattern and rubber soles to have the best grip if you want to avoid slipping on the court.

- **Cushioning**: Choose cushioned shoes that offer good support; otherwise, you could cause injury to your legs, feet, and ankles.

- **Breathable**: Your shoes should be breathable so your feet don't sweat and overheat.

- **Durability**: This goes without saying, but you need shoes that will last the distance. Good quality, strong shoes are more likely to withstand the inevitable wear and tear. The last thing you want is them falling apart on you after a couple of games.

- **Fit**: Ensure your shoes are comfortable with room to move your toes.

- **Support**: Your shoes should offer lateral support to keep your feet stable during movement on the court.

- **Flexibility**: The soles should be flexible to provide stability and traction and allow you to move freely and quickly.

- **Weight**: Choose lightweight shoes because if you wear heavy ones, you will tire quickly and find it hard to navigate the court quickly.

Your shoes are as important as everything else you need for Pickleball, especially those with leg and foot injuries or pain. For example, let's say you are a flat-footed player. In that case, the proper shoes are needed to keep your arches stable and reduce the risk of injury caused by the wrong posture.

The Pickleball Court

This is probably the most important part of Pickleball. Standard courts are 20 feet wide, 44 feet long, and divided in half equally by a net, which must run the full 20 feet width of the court. The net must be supported by posts at either end and should be 36 inches tall at the outer edges, dropping to 34 inches in the center.

All the lines painted on the court must be 2 inches wide and included in the 20 by 44 feet dimensions. They should also be strongly contrasting to the court's surface.

Learning to play the game requires an understanding of the zones and lines on the Pickleball court.

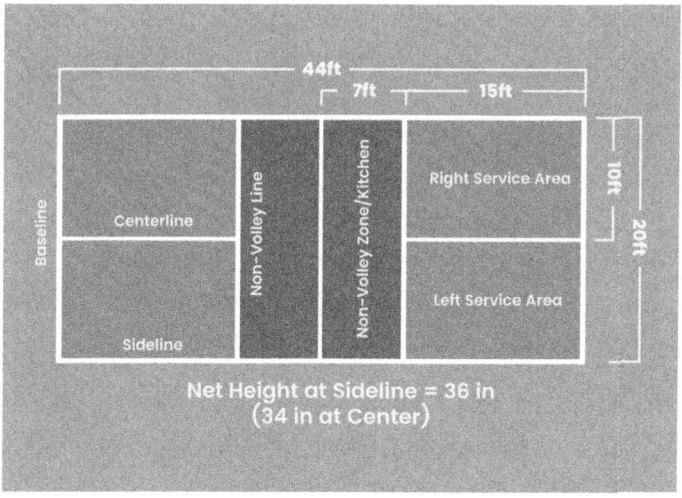

5. *Pickleball court with lines. Source: https://usaPickleball.org/wp-content/uploads/2020/06/PickleballCourtGraphic.png*

The Lines:

- **Baseline**: This is the back line and is on both sides. It indicates where the court ends, and it runs in a straight line parallel to the net. All players must serve from the baseline, and they cannot cross it during the serve. It marks the ends of the court and is parallel to the Pickleball net. It is where a player serves the ball from, creating a plane that the serving player cannot cross while serving.

- **Sidelines**: The lines running down the sides of the court. They run the full 44 feet, are perpendicular to the net, and mark the outer width boundaries.

- **Centerline**: Again, perpendicular to the net, this line keeps the odd and even courts separate. It is 15 feet long and runs between the baseline and non-volley line on both sides.

- **Non-Volley Line**: This is a 7-foot area parallel to the net on both sides and indicates where the non-volley zone's outer boundary is.

Zones:

- **Non-Volley Zone**: You'll mostly hear this referred to as the "kitchen" zone. It is the full width of the court and runs 7 feet back from the net on both sides. It is marked by the sidelines and non-volley lines and a volley in this zone is illegal. Neither can a server touch the lines or bounce the ball in the marked area.

- **Even and Odd Courts**: Also known as the left and right service areas, these are located at the back of each side of the court. They are marked by the centerline, sidelines, non-volley line, and baseline. As you stand facing the net, the odd court is left of the centerline, while the even court is right. These names help identify a server's position when playing doubles.

Best Pickleball Court Surfaces

Concrete and asphalt are widely considered the best surfaces as they produce good bounce and speed, but clay and grass are also becoming more popular.

- **Clay**: Usually red or green/gray clay, these are becoming very popular in the USA. Clay is a good surface, offering a good bounce and a faster-paced game.

- **Grass**: A recent addition, a grass court makes for a challenging game, especially in the kitchen zone, because it stops the ball from bouncing too much. When you play on grass, you can use different strategies to those used on traditional court surfaces.

Indoor courts are usually constructed of concrete or asphalt with a polyurethane or rubber coating on top.

A good court is the right size, has a good surface material, and has a properly fitted net. Yes, you can use popup courts for a quick game, but a permanent court ensures the rules are followed more closely and the game is played as it should be.

Lighting is a must if you want to play outdoors at night or on an indoor court. You can use LED or HID lights outdoors, but if you play indoors, you will need fluorescent lighting.

You will also need a rest area. Pickleball is a demanding game, and players must take a break. If using an outdoor court, ensure there are shaded areas where you can also store water and equipment.

Chapter 3: Mastering the Rules of Pickleball

Picking up a racquet and trying to play Pickleball is one thing, but you won't get anywhere unless you understand the game's rules. Thankfully, they are not difficult to learn, more so if you already play another racquet sport. The rules for Pickleball are loosely based on the rules for table tennis, squash, tennis, and badminton.

Serving Rules

Every Pickleball game starts with a serve, and that includes rallies. There are 3 rules that you always need to keep in mind:

Underhand Serve

6. *The underhand serve. Source: https://Pickleballkitchen.com/wp-content/uploads/2017/11/serve_upward.jpg*

In sports that are within the same scope, overhand serves are encouraged. However, with Pickleball, this is not the case. It's a golden rule that serves need to be underhand. The ball must not be hit from a position any higher than your navel; in other words, the ball and racquet make contact beneath this point:

- You can serve with either a backhand or forehand, but remember to always raise your arm to make contact with the ball.

- Ensure that your racquet is held in a way where the point at the highest position is below the joint bend on your wrist.

When your racquet has hit the ball, you can handle it in any way you want. This means your racquet doesn't have to be in a certain position to hit the ball once the serve has been hit.

Foot Placement

Before serving, have a look at how your feet are positioned. Right before the baseline, one foot needs to be placed firmly on the ground. Jumping while you serve is not allowed.

Your feet shouldn't come in contact with the centerline extensions, the imaginary sideline, or the baseline. Your feet must not be inside the baseline. After serving, though, there are no restrictions on where you can move on your side of the court.

Crosscourt Serve

When you serve, the ball must cross the net and settle in the crosscourt service area; whether it touches the net or not is irrelevant. The kitchen, sidelines, and baselines surround the crosscourt service area, which is the space directly across from the server on the other side of the court.

A fault occurs if the ball touches the kitchen line or the kitchen zone. It might, however, contact the base, center, or sidelines.

If you break any of these three regulations, your serve will be deemed invalid, and you will forfeit your rally.

Volley Serve/Drop Serve

In Pickleball, there are two ways to serve: the "volley serve" and the "drop serve."

The volley serve requires you to let go of the ball or throw it up and hit it without letting it bounce. This is considered the traditional way to serve, so here are a couple of tips to help you perfect it:

- Before you hit the ball, lift or throw it up. This provides the time and space you need to hit the ball firmly. While you must hit the ball while it is beneath your navel, this also allows you time to hit it at a higher point, i.e., not down by your knees.

- If you throw the ball and it isn't a good throw, do NOT hit the ball. Once you hit it, the ball is in play, and a bad throw could mean the difference between winning and losing the point. The rules state that you have 10 seconds to hit the ball, so let it fall to the ground, pick it up, and start again – just make sure you stay within the 10 seconds.

- Practice throwing the ball up. New rules for this year state that you cannot add spin to the throw before you hit it.

The other way is the drop serve. This was officially created for players with a physical disability, i.e., they only have one arm. That said, all players are now allowed to use it right now. To execute this serve, hold the ball at a natural height, i.e., not above your head! Drop it and let it bounce once before hitting it.

Both the drop and volley serves follow the same rules:

- No matter which serve type you choose, you can do it with a forehand or backhand.

- The foot placement rules are applicable to volley and drop serves.

- In the same way, the location rules are applicable to both – when you serve the ball, it must hit the ground in the correct crosscourt service area.

- You only have ten seconds to hit the ball after the score is announced, so make it count.

The limitations do not, however, apply to a drop serve. This means that you don't have to worry about only hitting the ball below your navel, about raising your arm, or about keeping the racquet below the point of the wrist joint. This is because a well-executed drop serve won't bounce higher than the navel. This indicates that you can apply backspin or sidespin to it; a volley serve does not permit you to do so. A serve with a lot of spin can be challenging to return, or it might be returned with forehand topspin, which is also a rare occurrence with a volley serve.

When to Serve

You must wait for the score to be called before you can hit the ball. In a singles match, the score is two digits, while in a doubles match, the score is three digits. Hitting the ball before the score is called will be considered a fault, which could cause you to lose the rally and point.

You must hit the ball within 10 seconds after the score is called. The 10-second rule must be followed even if your opponents are not in the right position or are not ready to receive. But the server or referee shouldn't announce the result before the receivers are prepared.

The exception to that rule is when the serving team is incorrectly positioned after the score has been called, and they move to the right position. In that case, the referee and/or serving team must give the server time to get into the right position, at which point the score is then called again, and the 10 seconds starts over.

A fault is called if either rule is violated, and the serve is thus lost.

Service Faults

A fault is called when the rules are violated in such a way that play is stopped, and the player or team that caused the fault loses the rally. According to the official rules, the following will result in such a fault:

Service Foot Fault: These are measured at the second a server's racquet touches the ball. There are a number of situations that could result in a malfunction at the point of contact, including:

- If at least one foot is behind the baseline and off the ground.

- If at least one foot touches or is inside the baseline.

- If at least one foot is outside or within the centerline or sideline extensions (imaginary).

- If the server is not standing in the right area when serving.

- If the wrong person serves the ball.

- The server uses an illegal motion when they serve the ball.

- If the ball doesn't land in the service court. This applies even when the ball hits the net or net cord. The service court covers the base, side, and centerlines but does not include the kitchen zone or line.

- The server makes contact with the ball before the entire score is called.

- Before the ball hits the ground, it hits something permanently positioned; the only exception to this is the net.

- The ball rebounds off the server or their partner, their racquet, or any part of their clothing.

- After striking the ball, the server or their partner requests a timeout or that the score be called.

No Service Lets

Play will continue if the ball strikes any portion of the net, including the cord, but only if it lands in the proper crosscourt location. Serves are never repeated because there are no service lets. Even after touching the net, a service fault occurs if the ball doesn't land on the ground properly.

Receiving Faults

The receiving team can also incur faults when returning the serve. In this case, the serving team earns a point. These scenarios include:

- If the ball is hit by the incorrect player on the receiving side.

- If the ball is touched by any player on the receiving team, even unintentionally, or the ball is interfered with before it can land. An example of this is if the ball hits the closest receiver to the net after being served or it is served long and hits the player on the other side of the receiver's baseline before it can bounce. In the latter case, the ball would normally have been out of bounds, but it incurs a receiver fault instead.

- A receiver fault occurs if the receiving team requests a timeout or requests that the score be confirmed after the server has already served.

Misunderstood Rules

While most rules are straightforward, some players usually misunderstand a few rules, usually beginner players. These rules are known as "other rules" in the official rule book. Any player who commits one of these will be penalized, and either they or their team will lose the rally. This means that even while they aren't "official" rules, you still need to understand them and know how to comply.

Double Hits

These are only legal under specific circumstances. To be considered legal, a hit must be:

- Unintentional.

- Continuous.

- A one-directional stroke.

- Hit by only one player.

If a double hit is intentional, non-continuous, goes in several directions, or more than one player hits the ball, a fault is declared, and the player loses the rally. Provided they are legal, a double hit is allowed on a serve.

Two-Handed Shots and Switching Hands

Missed Shots

You don't get a dead ball if you swing for it and miss. Instead, you keep playing until one of two things happens: the ball bounces twice before it is hit, or a player commits a fault. If you do miss the ball, keep playing and take another swipe at it. If you know you can't get it, you should signal your partner to have a go. However you do it, the ball must be hit before the second bounce. If not, and the ball is completely missed, it's a fault. If the ball is even lightly touched and it doesn't reach the other side of the court, a fault occurs when the ball lands or touches a permanent object.

Cracked/Broken Ball

If a ball breaks or cracks during a rally, the game must continue until the rally ends. At this point, the player can then ask for the ball to be looked at. Any other player or the referee can do this, and should a player ask for this, the following rules apply:

- When the game is being refereed by an official, it is down to the official to check the ball. If they determine it has been broken or cracked, a new ball is provided, and the rally is replayed. If not, the rally stands, and a new ball is supplied.

- When the game isn't being refereed, all players involved in the game must reach a consensus that a compromised ball played a part in how the rally ended. If yes, the rally is replayed using a different ball, but if the players cannot agree, the rally stands.

If there is no damage to the ball, play will continue, and the rally stands.

Injury During Gameplay

If a player is injured during gameplay, play must continue until the rally ends. However, if you are not playing in a tournament or competition, you can stop and deal with the injury before replaying the point if both teams agree. Do keep in mind that when your game is purely for fun, not all the official rules apply. If one of you is injured, you should stop and deal with it.

Equipment Problems

If a player loses a shoe or other piece of equipment or clothing or breaks their racquet, play must continue until the rally ends unless it results in a fault. Broken racquets or lost equipment/clothing can result in a fault in several ways, and some of the more common ways are:

- When a broken or damaged racquet or the item the player lost hits the ground in the non-volley zone before the ball bounces.

- When the broken or lost item goes over the net or touches the net, cords, or posts.

- When the broken or lost item causes a distraction to your opponents just as they are about to serve or return the ball.

Items on the Court

An item that isn't supposed to be on the court only incurs a fault if it is in the non-volley zone and was caused by a rally. Other than that, there is no fault. A fault is also not incurred if the ball in play hits the item. Consider a scenario in which something occurs on your side of the court but does not lead to a mistake. Play continues in that situation since the object didn't land in the non-volley zone. On the other hand, your rival returns the rally and strikes the object that landed on the court. According to the rules, play continues until the rally is completed.

However, should something land in the non-volley zone while a rally is ongoing, it incurs a non-volley fault. An example of this is if the ball is hit before it has bounced once. The object will not be penalized if it lands in the non-volley zone without being hit by a volley.

Net Plane

Another misunderstood rule revolved around the net plane. Many people believe that you cannot cross it before the ball is hit. The imaginary line known as the "net plane" extends the net past the net posts. Any apparel you wear or possessions you carry are subject to the rule. Strictly speaking, if you or any of your clothing or equipment crosses this line before you hit the ball, it results in a fault, and the rally is lost.

There are always exceptions, and this is no different. You are allowed to cross the net plane without making a mistake if the ball bounces with enough force or backspin to return across the court untouchable. Only once the ball has reached the opposing side of the court may you cross the plane to hit it. If you don't make contact with the ball, your opponents will score a point.

Remember, you can not touch the posts, net, or anything on the opposite side of the court as long as the ball is being played. Doing this may cause you to sustain a fault, and you will lose the rally.

Court Distractions

Distracting your opponents at the time of their serve is not allowed. If you do, you can incur a fault. Examples of this include shouting at them or doing anything that could distract them in any way. This will lose you the rally, and you will incur a fault.

A referee should be able to determine whether an opponent's rally loss was due to a distraction. All players should concur that the distraction costs the rally if there isn't a referee accessible. Players should consult a referee or the event director for advice if they are unable to reach a consensus.

One thing that is not considered a direction is communication between team partners. For example, you may tell a team member to watch out as the serve is made or to get back from the line. In this case, no fault is incurred, and play continues. This type of communication may be classed as a distraction in some cases. For example, if you enter the kitchen zone just as your opponent is about to play and yell at them to watch out, this could be classed as a distraction and would incur a fault.

Pickleball Coaching

Coaching in Pickleball is when a person other than the player's partner communicates with a player verbally, non-verbally, or in an electronic format with the aim of providing an advantage to the player. Coaching is only allowed between players on the same team. Anyone not playing can only provide coaching during timeouts and between games – no other time.

If a person is considered to be coaching a player for a competitive advantage, the referee will issue the player or team a technical warning. The team or player will be given a technical foul if it happens again during gameplay. This means they lose a point – if their score is already zero, a point is given to the other team or player.

Racquet Rules

You are only allowed to use a single racquet in a game, which means you can't change halfway through unless your racquet is damaged in a way that can't be used. Players must also be holding their racquet when hitting the ball; this means no throwing it at the ball in the hopes of hitting it. You will lose the rally and commit a fault if you break either of the rules.

Net and Net Post Rules

The ropes and cords that stretch between the posts and sidelines are considered part of the net. If the ball hits the net between these posts and makes it to the other side, it is still in play as long as no other fault has been committed. However, a foul is committed if the player or any of their clothing, gear, or posts come into contact with them. Hitting the ball between the net and the posts will incur a fault.

The posts, including their arms and wheels, are usually positioned out of bounds. This means that if a ball touches a post, it is considered out of bounds, causing the player to incur a fault and lose the rally. The same is true if a player, their equipment, or clothing touches the posts while the ball is in play.

Temporary Nets with Horizontal Bars

There are some rules surrounding these:

- The offending player loses the rally and receives a fault if the ball makes contact with the horizontal bar or center base before it crosses to the other side of the court.

- It is considered a let should the ball go over the net and:

  o Hits the bar or center base before or after it bounces, OR

  o Land somewhere between the net and bar, whether it bounces or not, and becomes trapped.

  If either of these happens, the point must be replayed. However, the exception to this is on the serve.

- On the serve, if the ball reaches the other side of the court before or after one of the scenarios listed above, it incurs a fault and a lost rally.

- Should a temporary net go wrong or break in the rally, the point is replayed.

Around the Posts Shots

You might hear these called ATPs, and they are legal shots in Pickleball. There is no rule that says the ball must go across the net. Instead, you may hit it around the net posts, but it must land on the other side and not be out of bounds. If you do hit one of these, you can hit the ball lower than the height of the net, but you cannot hit it, so it goes between the post and the net. This would incur a fault.

Chapter 4: Learning Racquet Techniques

Once you have mastered the rules, it's time to get to grips – literally – with the sport. Learning how to hold your racquet is critical because your grip affects your gameplay.

How to Grip a Pickleball Racquet

You can use one of three grip types, each with its pros and cons. Which one you choose depends on your playing style.

Eastern Grip

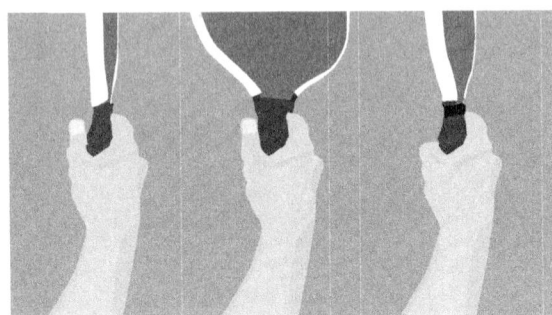

7.   Eastern grip. Source: https://dac8r2vkxfv8c.cloudfront.net/images/post/52ff-06-22-ImagesBlog_GripPaddle.jpg

This is the most common grip type and is much the same as how you would shake a person's hand or hold a hammer. Follow these steps:

1. Grip your racquet in your strongest hand (your dominant hand).

2. Place your palm on the racquet handle with your index finger resting on the third bevel.

This is a good grip for beginners because it is firm, making racquet control much easier. However, it is nowhere near as powerful as the other grip types.

Western Grip

8.   Western grip. Source:
https://cdn.sanity.io/images/jvolei4i/production/4ba330db656fd7
27e48e31289c3f88ff53b142b7-2000x1332.png

Also popular, the Western grip is similar to holding a tennis racquet. Do it like this:

1.   Grip your racquet in your strongest hand.

2. Grip the racquet handle with your hand and rest your index finger against the first bevel on the handle.

3. Ensure your fingers wrap around the handle and your index finger and thumb face each other – one on either side of the handle.

This grip provides spin and power but is not the easiest to master.

Continental Grip

9. Continental grip. Source:
https://cdn.sanity.io/images/jvolei4i/production/e58b8d06039bd
8739ecfb205d47378b95101922b-2000x1332.png

Not used as much, the Continental grip is similar to the Eastern, but your index finger is closer to the racquet's head. Do this:

1. Grip the racquet in your strongest hand.

2. Your hand should be on the racquet handle, and your index knuckle should be resting on the second bevel.

---

3. Wrap your fingers around the handle, ensuring your thumb and index finger are on either side, facing each other.

This grip works for net play but doesn't have the power of the other two grips.

Improving Your Grip

Use the tips below to improve your control:

1. **Choose the Right Grip:** As you saw, you can choose from one of the three main grips. Practice all of them and choose what feels comfortable to you.

2. **Adjust:** Depending on your shot, your grip may need adjusting. Let's say you hit a forehand shot. You might need to adjust your wrist slightly to the right so you can hit the ball cleanly. You might need to turn it left a little for a backhand shot. The key is to experiment and find the best grip for you.

3. **Practice:** This is the only way to get comfortable, so practice holding your racquet without playing or hitting a ball. This ensures muscle memory develops, and you learn the balance and weight of your racquet. Practice holding your racquet out in front of you. Then, practice holding it over your head and out to either side. You must be comfortable in any position.

4. **Relax:** If you grip the racquet too tight, it creates tension in your arm and wrist, negatively affecting your game. Relax and hold the racquet a little looser but firmly – it must be comfortable above all else. This will give you better control without losing accuracy or power.

5. **Focus:** Grip is all-important, but so is focusing on the ball. In time, picking up and holding your racquet will become automatic. This leaves you free to focus your attention on where the ball goes and the shot you choose to make. Try to watch the ball all the time and adjust your grip as required.

Top Tips on Holding Your Racquet

These tips are designed to ensure maximum comfort, control, and focus:

- **Hold It with Both Hands:** Most people use one hand, but using both gives you more control. Your weakest hand should always be used to keep the racquet steady and aim your shot. Make sure it is located above your strongest hand when you hold the racquet. Your strong hand will provide support when you need it.

- **Find the Sweet Spot:** Every Pickleball racquet has this sweet spot. It is the part of the racquet head that provides the most power and accurate shots. Finding it means practicing hitting the ball with different parts of the head. When you find it, you'll know because the ball will fly with power and accuracy.

- **Vary Your Pressure:** You should always use a firm grip on your racquet, but you can vary it to make different shots. For example, if you execute a softer drop shot, your grip should be loose, while you need to hold the racquet more tightly if for a hard drive shot.

- **Don't Hold It Low or High:** Doing so can affect the power and trajectory of your shot. Try to hold the racquet at waist height, extending your arm a little, giving you accuracy and power while retaining control.

- **Regular Practice:** The more practice you get at holding your racquet, the easier it will be to get the grip right and adjust when needed. Without using a ball, take the time to practice with grips, grip pressure, and finding the sweet spot. If you practice consistently, your game will improve, and you can have even more fun.

Importance of Correct Racquet Handling

Learning to hold your racquet properly is critical to playing a good game of Pickleball, and there are several reasons why:

- **Control:** Proper grip gives you more control. A loose grip can lead to the racquet moving in your hands, resulting in inconsistent, sloppy shots. If your grip is tight, your arm and wrist will tense up, affecting your control and accuracy.

- **Power:** Proper grip gives your shots more power. The correct grip on your racquet provides energy, and your shots will be more powerful.

- **Comfort:** If you don't hold the racquet correctly, your wrist, arm, and hand could become painful and uncomfortable. A proper grip eliminates that risk, and you can play for longer.

- **Prevention of Injuries:** An incorrect grip can lead to your muscles and joints becoming stressed, leading to injuries. Holding your racquet the right way reduces these risks.

- **Variety of Shots:** You can change your shot type depending on your grip. For example, a looser grip helps with softer drop shots, while a tighter grip enables better hard drives. When you can learn the different grips, you can use different shots in your game, making you a better player.

Holding your racquet right can ensure you play properly and can also help you win the game. Incorrect grip can lead to you losing every point and the game. Make sure you choose the right grip for how you play, practice the correct grip, and learn how to adjust it to switch between styles.

Let's look at some Pickleball shots.

The Basics of Pickleball Shots

There are six basic shots in Pickleball, and these will discussed now.

The Serve

The serve sets the tone for a rally and is the basis of every point in a game. The one shot you can completely control is your serve, so you need to have one that is dependable and consistent. There are also five critical rules a player must learn, which were already covered earlier. Two of the most important are:

- **Placement and Control**: Underhand serves are a rule of the game, and contact between the ball and racquet must occur below the navel – accuracy is more important than the spin or speed.

- **Grip, Positioning, and Footwork:** Ensuring the right grip, foot placement, and body technique will result in a strong serve. If you are consistent, your serve will be better placed, no matter where you aim for, and your opponent will struggle to work out where you are going next. That makes it much harder for them to vary their shots to gain the upper hand.

The Dink

The dink is a critical shot in Pickleball, and it requires no small measure of precision and control. It is one of the softer shots in the game, and you always execute it close to or at the net. Done correctly, this shot can outsmart your opponent, and it can help slow the game down. The dink should be used when your opponents are expecting a hard shot with plenty of power. They won't see it coming, and it causes confusion – exactly what you need to win. Performed right, the dink will fly upwards and drop gently over the net into their no-volley zone.

If you can master the dink, it can improve your strategy, allowing you to control where the ball goes during gameplay. It also puts your opponents under pressure to return a challenging ball or lose points.

Not only is it one of the best shots you can master, but learning the dink shot is important to learning and understanding the other shots. Get your grip, footwork, and swing techniques right, and practice your drills, and you are ready to face the game, no matter what comes up. Focus your attention on consistency and accuracy, practice adding some variation to your dinks, and you'll have all the flexibility you need to play against someone with more experience and skill than you.

The Drive

10. The drive. Source: https://1.bp.blogspot.com/-Auxd_EBe-gc/VnC-ksOsLuI/AAAAAAAAAic/badEmPsSKGk/s1600/thirdshot3.png

Another critical Pickleball shot is the drive; you can win points by hitting the ball fast and hard against the opposing team. Whether a groundstroke or volley is employed determines how a drive shot is executed. If the ball has bounced, the forehand drive is made with little to no arc. This is an effective shot when you play people who like to rally hard shots at you.

That said, this shot can only be successfully executed if your footwork and body positioning are correct. You also need to ensure you stay on balance when you swing your racquet. Relax and extend your racquet out fully to follow through.

The Lob

This is one of the most important shots. If hit correctly, it will send the ball flying high above your opponent. You must use a high-to-low arm motion and ensure that the ball is hit at the bottom. This will give the shot plenty of backspin and loft. Using the lob makes your opponent get off the kitchen line, giving you all the time and space you need to get on the offensive.

To shoot an effective lob shot, you should target your opponent's weaker side. Getting your opponent to move from their comfort zone can help you win a lot of points. For example, aim for a player's backhand if they have a strong forehand. Playing a few well-placed lobs significantly increases your chances of winning.

The Drop Shot

A drop shot is considered a delicate shot because you hit the ball softly off the bounce. Mastering this shot can significantly improve your game. Hit it right, and it should land in your opponent's non-volley zone. Players often hit this shot from the baseline, making their opponents move forward.

That said, perfecting the drop shot will take a great deal of skill and practice. Even pro players struggle with consistent execution. However, only consistent execution can push you up the ranks from beginner to pro level, allowing you more control and precision during a rally.

The Block

Learning the block shot is crucial to helping you stop your opponent from gaining the upper hand with a strong third-shot drive. The block shot requires you to have quick reactions, exceptional hand-eye coordination, and the ability to control the power of your shots so you don't hit the shot too soft or hard. This is one of those shots where practice really does make perfect.

So, how do you master this shot? First, you need great positioning and footwork because you need to be able to anticipate the shot and get into the right place. You also need the right grip on your racquet, too, as this will allow you to control where the ball goes while you block those shots throughout the game.

Advanced Pickleball Shots

Once you have mastered the basic shots, you can move on to more advanced shots to shake your game up even more.

The Third Shot Drop

11. The third shot drop. Source: https://4.bp.blogspot.com/-A_mF9pdZgVo/VnCq2o__UKI/AAAAAAAAAiA/F3hRQLJlm-c/s1600/thirdshot2.png

This essential technique is one that every player should learn. The third drop should land in your opponent's kitchen zone and is hit softly close to the baseline. Doing this successfully limits how much your opponent can attack, so it is a critical shot to learn. Mastering this can ensure your team is set up for a great offensive game while preventing attacks from your opponent.

You can use several strategies to keep your opponents on their toes, and the best one is to vary your shots, adding in a third shot drop every now and again to keep things interesting. The less predictable you are, the harder it is for them to determine their moves in advance. Mastering this shot gives you control over the game and more chances of scoring points.

The Forehand

This is one of the more important shots, but it will take a significant amount of practice to master. The forehand drive works well on groundstrokes and swinging volleys, making it a versatile shot.

You need power, balance, and accuracy to execute this properly, and your focus must be on your footwork. An open stance is required when you approach the ball. You must also have a firm grip on your racquet so your shot is delivered with the most power while controlling its direction.

The Backhand

The backhand is quite a difficult shot, but you must learn how to use it with volleys and groundstrokes. It requires using a continental grip, angling your racquet up slightly, and providing power by stepping into the ball.

A backhand punch shot is even more challenging but another great shot to learn. It requires you to hit the ball fast and precisely toward your opponent while putting a spin on it. If you can do this, you gain better accuracy and control over your game while adding some variety to your tactics.

The Volley

This advanced technique requires you to have quick reflexes and precise timing. It's an incredibly powerful shot that can quickly end the points, and the key is correct body positioning, footwork, and racquet placement.

To execute volleys properly, you need to hold the racquet correctly. Position it above your wrist, as this gives you more control over the direction of the ball and more precision on where it lands. Most Pickleball volleys are done near the net because this position takes advantage of poor returns. Good volleys can make your opponent move and could result in them making mistakes that lead to you winning the point.

The Smash

This advanced shot needs agility, precision, and speed. It is an overhand shot, incredibly hard to master that you must fire downwards into the opposite court. The idea is to gain control and quickly end the point.

Footwork and body positioning are crucial to master for this shot, as they help you get to your position, and swing is important to smash the ball up and over, hopefully catching your opponents on the hop. This will take time to perfect, but you can improve your consistency and accuracy with practice.

The Slice

Also called the chop shot, this advanced technique can be used on returns and serves. Use a low or high motion to put a spin on the ball, causing it to change direction in midair by curving.

This is one of the best shots to use when varying your gameplay. Because your opponents will never know which direction your ball is heading, it can give you a great advantage. Mastery of this shot requires that you practice turning your shoulder to face the ball. This is another shot that requires a lot of practice to get it right.

The Importance of Shot Technique

Pickleball shot technique is crucial for the following reasons:

Improving Control and Accuracy

The shot technique can improve the accuracy of your shots. Learning shot placement is critical to this. This means aiming for specific parts of the court that will make your opponent struggle to return the ball, i.e., deep corners or sidelines. Your odds of winning increase if you aim the ball to the right of your opponent.

Gaining accuracy and control can also be accomplished by using the third drop shot. When you make these delicate, accurate strokes that land in the kitchen zone, your opponent will be forced to volley the ball upwards, giving you more time and space to seize the initiative.

Increasing Power and Speed

Pickleball requires strength and speed to master. You can accomplish this by putting your body in the right position and picking your shots wisely. You can increase power while maintaining control, for instance, by using a topspin shot.

Learning speed and power requires you to learn body positioning and timing. The right weight transfer with a properly executed swing will provide great power to your shot. To help with speed, take the time to practice agility.

Achieving Consistency

Successful games require you to be consistent in your shots. First, learn all the basic shots and become proficient at them. Then, you can start learning advanced techniques and teaching yourself to be consistent. Doing so gives you more control over your shots and accuracy in practice games and real ones.

Making sure your footwork is perfect is one key to consistency. Your shots will be executed properly if your feet are quick and accurate. Also, make sure you work on body positioning. This can help you make sure that your shots are successful.

Using Shot Drills

Shot drills can help you take your skills to the next level. The drills below will help you improve your speed, consistency, and power if you do them regularly.

Continuous Dinking Drill

This is one of the most important drills to help you improve your game. The continuous dinking drill can help you learn low, slow shots, which are necessary for maintaining a long dinking rally. The aim is to learn to keep the ball going for as long as possible with no mistakes.

This drill does require you to practice dinks with a partner over a short distance. When you master it, challenge yourself by increasing the distance, speed, and difficulty of the shots. Push yourself hard, as this is the only way you will learn and improve. The benefits of this drill include challenging you to keep your focus under challenging conditions, thus improving your mental agility and stamina during gameplay.

Groundstroke Consistency Drill

Mastering this drill is also important to game mastery. It helps you improve your footwork, groundstrokes, and consistency; you must stay in one position on the court and hit multiple crosscourt shots.

You will focus on shot consistency and getting your shots to land in specific parts of the court. When you practice regularly, your groundstrokes will improve in accuracy and control. You will find it much easier to read your opponent and anticipate and react to their shots more precisely. This requires you to learn the right technique to focus on your footwork, racquet grip and control, the sweet spot, and improving your coordination, especially hand-eye.

Lob Shot Accuracy Drill

This is one of the most important drills for improving defensive play. If you can master it, you give yourself plenty of time to set your offensive game up. Practice hitting lobs continuously over a pole or net. Make sure you aim for a certain point on the opposite side.

Integrating this drill into your practice is recommended to help you improve certain techniques needed in gameplay. This includes improving the accuracy of your lob shots while attacking out-of-place or off-balance opponents or those who tend to mis-hit quite a lot.

Smash Power Drill

This is a crucial drill for developing your skills, and it focuses on improving your smash shot, giving it more accuracy and power. To execute a smash shot, you need to be able to hit the ball fast and hard to win points.

To practice this, stand on the baseline. Ask someone to serve the ball crosscourt and smash it back. Practice this to ensure your hand-eye coordination is the best it can be. It will also help you practice hitting hard shots and improve your accuracy, speed, and power.

One more thing this drill can do is help you become more consistent with your smash shots; master it, and you'll have more opportunities to win. It also builds strength in your core muscles, arms, and shoulders, which gives your shots more power.

Becoming proficient with your shot techniques will make you a much better player. Learn the basic shots and then move on to mastering the more advanced ones to gain the best advantage you can have.

The techniques help you improve your control, power, accuracy, speed, and consistency. However, these techniques are about much more. They sharpen your skills at anticipating your opponent's every move and help you adapt your position to get the best shot. And when you learn so many different shots, you can begin to vary them in your gameplay, thus putting your opponent off their stride.

The shot drills are carefully designed to help you improve certain techniques and skills, and adding them to your training will ensure you are a better player, more adaptable to every situation, and better able to read the game and respond in a way that wins you the points. The most important thing to improve your game is practice and a lot of it.

Chapter 5: Navigating the Pickleball Court

Let's move on and fine-tune your court techniques by talking about your positioning and navigation around the Pickleball court. Learning body positioning is incredibly important. It doesn't matter how many great shots you perfect. Not being able to position yourself correctly, let alone move in the right way, means you won't have any control over shots.

Learning positioning on the court and in your body will allow everything to come together, and you'll find the game much easier to grasp.

We'll start by discussing the best positions on the court, including body and feet, and then we'll discuss positioning concerning your racquet and other equipment and ways to move about the court.

Body Positions

A critical aspect of Pickleball is holding yourself in the right position. You will lose any advantage in the game if your footwork and body positioning are not right. It's crucial to delve into the right body positioning, from the feet upward, and some people term this as the "ready" position.

Footing

How you position your feet is as important as where you stand on the court. All players understand that footwork is important, regardless of what sport they play and that applies to Pickleball too. So, what is the optimal foot position for the best gameplay?

The best position is with your feet apart, about shoulder-width is enough. This makes you more flexible and able to move quickly when needed, and it gives you the stability you need to avoid falling over or tripping. If your feet are too close together, you won't be able to balance very easily, so try not to do it. When you stand with your feet apart, you are ready to jump and run at will, something you need to do a lot on a Pickleball court.

You should also point your toes slightly outward, as this allows you a better grip on the ground, and it will be easier to jump into action when needed.

Get plenty of practice in standing properly, and when you are sure you have it right, you can move on.

Legs and Knees

When your foot positioning is correct, you need to work on your knees and legs. Getting their positioning right means reducing the risk of injury. The best position is to keep your knees slightly bent to give you a bit more bounce and flexibility. Do not lock your knees; it will only end in pain.

Having your knees bent allows you to be ready to make sudden movements and works well with your foot placement.

Now, practice getting your foot stance correct with your leg and knee placement.

Arms and Torso

Lastly, the arms and torso. There is more to Pickleball than your legs and feet; you need to use your whole body. Lean forward slightly – if you have your knee and foot placement correct, this shouldn't be difficult. Leaning forward engages your glutes and puts you in a position to move fast when needed.

Holding your racquet, extend your arms in front of you. Lean forward a little, putting most of your weight onto your toes.

Practice, practice, practice. Get this stance correct, and you'll find it easy to move about the Pickleball court.

Moving Around the Court

Once you get to grips with your position, you can learn how to move on the Pickleball court. Like your foot and body position, how you move is also important, perhaps more so than where you move.

You need to think about a few things. First and most important is safety. While Pickleball is quite safe, if an accident can happen, it will. That means it is crucial to be on your guard at all times, and you must make sure that your movements don't cause any other players or you any danger.

Second, efficiency is also important. Because this is such a competitive game, all your movements need to be efficient and effective, giving you an advantage you must use to win the game. As such, optimization is the name of the game in movement. Let's now discuss some movement methods on the Pickleball court and how to get them into your game strategy.

The Split Step

12. The split step. Source:
https://i.ytimg.com/vi/wRFRSj0JI10/maxresdefault.jpg

A basic Pickleball movement is the split step; however basic it may be, it is important to learn. In the split step, you move by kind of leaping to get to your position. Because the court is usually small, you can normally get from one side to the other in just a couple of steps. This means you can reach shots you wouldn't be able to reach in any other similar game on a bigger court. As such, mastering this step will boost your game, giving you great flexibility in reaching all types of shots.

So, when should the split step be used?

Most players use the split step for two points: the first is when the opponent hits the ball, the second is after your initial serve, and you go to the kitchen line.

In the first case, the split step needs to be started the second the ball is hit. This will give you every opportunity to quickly decide your direction.

In the second case, the split step lets you get to the kitchen line relatively quickly and easily after your initial serve.

Practice the split step in both contexts until perfect, then move on to the next.

Move with No Pattern

A famous James Herbert book, Dune, was also made into a movie. In the movie, the characters must cross a desert, but dangerous worms beneath the sand get in the way. These worms can sense when the humans move, so the characters work their way across the sand in a way that doesn't involve patterns, making it harder for the worms to detect them.

Pickleball follows the same principles. If your patterns are random, your opponent won't know what to expect. The element of surprise is always your best bet; irregular and spontaneous movements will keep your opponents on their toes and on the back foot, unable to predict where you will go.

A word of caution – if you are playing a doubles match, make sure you and your teammate coordinate beforehand; the element of surprise is great to knock your opponent off their track but not your own team members!

Move at the Last Second

If your opponent is an excellent player, they will anticipate what you will do and make their shots to force you into a specific movement. So, what do you do? It's quite simple; you do whatever it takes to throw your opponent off guard so they can't work out what you are going to do.

This is best done by waiting until the last second to move. That way, your opponent won't detect your intention until it's happening. Of course, this also allows you to change your mind. There is no need to make your mind up about what to do; simply wait, see where the game is going, and then decide.

You could also fake your movements. For example, you might see some players leaning in one direction, making their opponent believe that's where they are going, and then going in a different direction at the last second. Or face one area of your opponent's court and hit the ball in the other direction. However, misdirection like this requires you to understand how to move on the court safely and fully practice that basic movements before trying anything more complicated.

Chapter 6: Court Etiquette and Sportsmanship

Please do not skip this chapter or skim it, as court etiquette is important to enjoyable play.

When did you last get an invite to a party? How did it feel, knowing you didn't know many people there? Did you feel jittery? Excited? Did your stomach feel like it was full of butterflies? That's exactly how your first game will make you feel. It's thrilling, with a healthy mix of worry thrown in.

13. Pickleball is a social game. Source:
https://unsplash.com/photos/UHZ_w1bOIvY?utm_source=unsplas
h&utm_medium=referral&utm_content=creditShareLink

Pickleball is one of the most social games, with some incredibly friendly and welcoming players. Because of that, if you mess up, it doesn't matter – no one will laugh at you. However, while the game is social, you still need to learn and understand a few unspoken rules regarding sportsmanship and etiquette. These are the most important ones to understand:

- You must own up to fouls.
- Give your opponents the benefit of the doubt.
- If you are wrong, admit to it and apologize.
- Be modest in your celebrations.
- Call for outs.
- Equal opportunity is important.
- Greet your opponents.
- Respect ball ownership.
- Retrieve the ball in safety.
- Share the courts.
- Tell others about stray balls.

Let's be clear here. While the aim of the game is to win, it isn't all about long drives and amazing drop shots. Pickleball works best with friendly players who are there to have fun and who abide by the unwritten sportsmanship rules.

This chapter walks you through the etiquette of Pickleball, including courtesy and tips that will definitely earn you some respect on the court.

Ball Etiquette

This relates to how players should manage ball-related issues. You may not always have control over where the ball goes, but you should know how to control whatever arises from the path it may take.

1. Respect Ball Ownership:

It won't take you long to realize that the Pickleball ball has a mind of its own. It might land on the court you play on or end up on another court altogether. That's just part of the game, and handling problems tactfully as they arise is important.

For example, if a stray ball lands on your court, return it where it came from; don't try to switch it with yours! Ball ownership is one of the more important etiquette rules in Pickleball, and proper etiquette dictates that you return the balls.

2. Retrieve the Ball in Safety

If a ball from another court lands on yours, do not stop your game, pick it up, and throw it back. Yes, its owner wants it back, but this isn't the best or safest way to get it back to them. The other players won't thank you for it, either. Not only that, but it could hit someone.

First, finish your rally and then pick the ball up. Then, see if you can spot its owner. If you can, make eye contact and nod at them to indicate the ball is on the way back. Then gently roll it across to them.

3. Tell Others about Stray Balls

Of course, if your ball goes astray, shout quickly, "Ball on the court!" and other players will know to look out for it. You will also warn them to avoid stepping on it or tripping over it and risking injury.

4. Understand Racquet Placement

New players might struggle a little with the racquet holder ritual. Don't worry; you haven't joined some strange, secret society; this is just how players track which player is up next. It works like this. A player will position their racquet on this holder, with an indicator telling others that they are the next player on the court. New players often forget to do this or they get the order in a muddle so no one knows who is playing next. If you are playing in a new court, check for these holders first and book your own place on the court by putting your racquet on one. If you are struggling to understand, ask someone. All the other players are more than happy to help you.

Pickleball Sportsmanship

This applies to all sports; sportsmanship is about generosity and fairness toward other players, putting your experience above all else instead of going all out to win the game, regardless of everyone and everything around you. Pickleball has several unwritten rules surrounding sportsmanship; you would do well to learn and remember them during gameplay.

1. Involve Everyone

Because Pickleball is so social, there are no limits on who can play. Nobody should be excluded because of their age, gender, skills, or any other reason. Pro players must expect to play beginners or intermediate players, and beginners should be happy to play and learn from someone with more experience.

The same rule applies to those with a physical advantage/disadvantage. If your opponent is physically limited in some way, you must not use that for your gain. At the end of the game, the game was originally developed as a way for people to come together and have fun, and regardless of whether you are a professional player or not, that still stands.

2. Play It Out

Sometimes, a game can get a bit heated, and that can lead to uncertainty. Was a foul shot played? Did the ball cross over the line? In situations like this, you should allow the benefit of the doubt. Pickleball is meant to be fun, so enjoy yourself and don't get hung up on the small stuff. Forgive and forget if there's a good chance the mistake was an accident.

3. Call the Shots

Even though Pickleball courts are relatively small in comparison to other sports, players still need to rely on their other competitors to make decisions. If you're uncertain whether your shot was in or out, trust your opponent to call it fairly. If you can see their shots, you should call in or out and follow suit. Give the other player the benefit of the doubt if you are unsure. This is reasonable and disadvantages no player.

4. Everyone Makes Mistakes

Players are only human at the end of the day. Own up if you do something wrong. Even if your toe was only a smidgeon over the kitchen line during a volley – that still counts as a rule violation. Integrity is king, and even if no one else sees you do it, own up.

And if you see another player do something wrong, point it out, but do it quietly and calmly, with little fuss. That way, the game is kept light and fun. The last thing you want is for everyone to spend their time micro-analyzing one another! That takes all the fun out of it.

5. Share the Court

Almost all Pickleball is played for fun, while only a small percentage is played in a tournament setting, although that is beginning to increase. This is why it should be kept as sociable and fun as it can be. So, while you may be busy enjoying the game, don't forget to break occasionally and let other people use the court.

Even as a beginner, it won't take you long to realize that all players like others to join in the fun, and it's one of the main reasons Pickleball is growing into such a popular game.

But if you don't share the court with others, everything will fall apart, and new players will find it difficult to pick up the game if no one lets them play. By engaging in conversation with other players during your break, you might just discover a new doubles partner or, at the very least, learn some useful advice.

6. Keep the Playing Field Level

Every Pickleball player enjoys a fast-paced dink rally, but if you are an expert playing a novice, you might want to consider slowing things down a little bit to keep your opponent in the game. And if you're a novice, don't forget to express gratitude to your professional opponent for being so gracious.

This shouldn't happen in tournaments, as players are typically placed into categories based on skill.

7. Keep Things Friendly

The Pickleball community thrives on the social aspect of playing as much as they do the actual game. When you go to play, keep things friendly by greeting other players and saying goodbye when you leave. Don't forget to congratulate others on their game, too.

Fostering a friendly game culture helps keep it casual and fun and ensures everyone can enjoy it, even when things get a little heated on the court. Most players are there for a fun workout and a bit of a social time. They don't want players who are so competitive that they forget the social niceties and put winning above all else.

It's simple: when you start a game, introduce yourself to the other players, shake hands, bump your fists, or even touch your racquets together. Anything that indicates you are being friendly; just be sure to thank them after the game.

8. Be Mindful When Celebrating

If you score a point, go ahead and celebrate – maybe a fist pump or you and your partner touching racquets. After all, you worked hard to win the point in what can be one of the trickiest games, so you should be happy and you should congratulate your partner. However, don't go overboard.

Don't go sliding across the court on your knees, arms thrown in the air, cheering! Don't run around the court screaming – that's for the soccer pitch! Just be mindful of everyone else around you and keep things light.

9. Keep Things Positive

Pickleball is a sport for everyone, so keep the bad vibes and trash talk out of it. You should also avoid being harsh with another player and not be too competitive; this spoils the game for everyone, and no one will think any better of you. Quite the opposite, in fact. If you have a tendency to lose your temper when something goes wrong, you should perhaps think about playing a different game, especially if you cannot get it out of your system before the game. Pickleball should be light, fun, and positive.

Court Etiquette

There's more to Pickleball than volleys and serves. You must also learn the court dance that keeps the game moving.

1. Don't Cross Too Early

This is about physically navigating from one side of the court to the other, not about cross-court dinking. It's all in the timing. You might want to say hi to a friend playing on a court beside you, but crossing the court without a thought for the other players is frowned upon. Wait until there's a break in the game, nod your hello to your friend, and continue playing. It's safer, and it reduces frustration and irritation.

2. Learn the Court Rhythm

Playing Pickleball is like going to a concert – you need to know when it's okay to take center stage and when to let others take the spotlight. This means you need to understand two things:

- Be alert. When it's your turn, get out there and play. Time wasters have no place on the Pickleball court.

- When your game is over, leave the court so other people can play their game. Don't hang around.

Abiding by this means everyone gets to enjoy their game.

3. Label Your Racquet

This is the best way to ensure your racquet stays yours. It avoids any mix-ups over who owns what racquet and eliminates the issues of not knowing who is playing next. All you need to do is put your initial on the grip. Do NOT mark the edge guard or racquet head.

4. Keep Power Play Under Control

It's great to see players going at a game with enthusiasm, but Pickleball isn't about who has the hardest swing. When you get a bit overzealous, people can end up getting hurt, or you may interrupt other games going on. It won't do your reputation any good either!

Keep things cool. Smashes are great, but not when they result in collisions and injury, and safety always comes first on the Pickleball court, and it's more important than winning a point.

Honing Your Skills

Pickleball is the kind of game that keeps you alert. Each game will bring something new; you'll learn different techniques and get to grips with the game's rules. The last two unwritten rules are kind of part of the etiquette rules and must be understood.

1. Know the Game Inside Out

The newbies and pro players are separated by one line – the pros perform a sleek dance with the game's rules. Beginners tend to fumble to start with and make mistakes that no pro player would make – even though they probably made the same ones when they were learning. What you need to do is understand the rules and make sure your game is played to them.

However, you don't need to have a study period every day to read and learn those rules, but you must ensure you know and understand them. Watch matches and see how the rules are played out in real time – this is a great source of help. You'll see your game improve as you learn the rules, and your partners will enjoy playing with you.

2. Never Stop Learning

Pickleball is a constantly changing game, and some of you will have been playing for a while, while others are just making their first foray onto the court. The important thing is to consider each match a lesson, each new opponent your teacher, and the whole experience as a learning curve.

If your game doesn't go particularly well, don't worry about it. Instead, learn from your mistakes and move on. If you have more experience than your opponent, don't be critical of them if they do something wrong. Take the opportunity to impart some of your hard-won knowledge and help them. Remember, you were there once.

Pickleball doesn't have the status of many other sports, but its love of sportsmanship and etiquette puts it on an equal footing with all of them. By learning and playing by the etiquette and sportsmanship rules, you are more than just a player. You belong to a fun-loving community of people who want nothing more than to welcome you into the fold.

Chapter 7: Scoring Strategies

Pickleball is a unique game that provides all ages of players and those of differing skill levels a fantastic experience. That said, while the rules must be learned and understood, as must playing techniques, scoring is one of the more critical areas all players must understand. When you do, you'll find the game offers more enjoyment and allows you to think up some better strategies to win.

This comprehensive chapter will help you untangle the mysteries of scoring and help you learn to understand it easily.

Understanding Pickleball Scoring

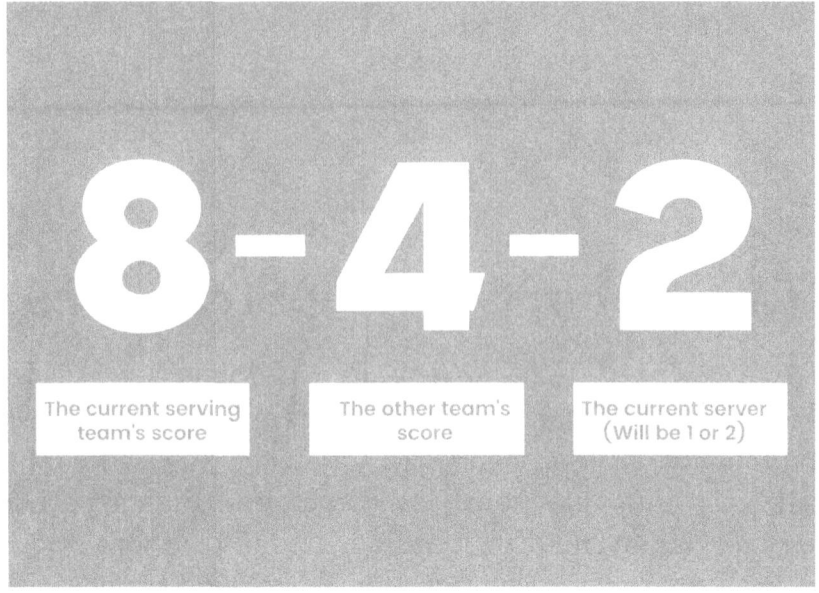

14. *Pickleball scoring. Source: https://Pickleballkitchen.com/wp-content/uploads/2018/05/scoreExplained1.jpg*

The scoring system in Pickleball awards players and teams for playing a fair game and winning rallies. Mostly, the scoring system is called rally scoring, which allows both teams to score. Traditional scoring only allows the serving team to win. The book will cover rally scoring later, but first, take a look at all the scoring rules as you need to learn these. If you don't, you might just find yourself on a losing streak, even if you feel the game should have been yours.

Basics of Pickleball Scoring

If you play a doubles match, the score consists of three numbers, i.e., 0-2-2. Those numbers mean:

- **The First Number:** The score for the serving team

- **The Second Number:** The score for the receiving team

- **The Third Number:** The score for the server, Server 1 or Server 2.

For example, let's say the score is 10-8-2; the serving team has scored 10, the receiving team is 8, and the serving team is on the second serve.

Singles Pickleball scoring only has two numbers, i.e., 0-1, broken down as:

- **The First Number:** The server's score

- **The Second Number:** The receiver's score.

Note that there is no third number here. That's because, in a singles games, there is only one serve for each team. So, if a score of 8:6 is called, the server scored 8, while the receiver scored 6.

In traditional scoring, points are scored ONLY for a serving team. The exception to this is when a technical fault has been called against the opponent, and the opponent's team hasn't scored yet. This applies whether the game is a doubles or singles match. If the serving team doesn't win the rally, they won't win the point.

The person or team who scores the winning point is the winner. A game will typically go to 11 points with a 2-point winning margin. In contrast, you can go to 15 or 21 points in a competition with a 2-point margin.

Player Positioning for Doubles Pickleball

In a doubles game, there are four serves in total, one from each player on each team. There is one exception to this; the team who serves first in a match will only get one serve. So, for a doubles game, the correct score at the start is 0-0-2.:

- 0: The first serving team

- 0: The receiving team

- 2: For the second server. If the team commits a fault or loses, there is a timeout, and the opposing team takes the rally.

Serves are delivered crosscourt, or in a diagonal motion. The serve normally starts on the right side of the serving team's court, which is the even side, and is sent diagonally to the even side of the receiving team's opponent.

The first server is referred to as Server 1, and the first serve is always delivered on the even side of the court. If the serving team wins the serve, they keep it and change sides. The first server must serve crosscourt once again. Only when a serve is successful do players switch courtsides, and only during serves. Until their team commits a mistake or the rally is lost, Server 1 keeps the serve.

Server 1 maintains the serve until the team makes a mistake or falls behind in the rally to their adversaries. In either case, the server forfeits their serve, and Server 2 from the same team takes over. The serve stays with the serving team once again until they lose the rally or make a mistake. A side-out is called, and the serve goes to the opponents if both members of the serving team miss their serves.

It is crucial that the players on the serving team know where each player is at the time of the serve and when it is returned. The player who serves has to be on the correct portion of the court, as must the receiving player. That portion of the court, i.e., even or odd, is decided by the score:

- **Even Score:** If the score is even numbers, i.e., 2, 4, 6, the starting player stays on the right-hand side of the court.

- **Odd Score:** If the score is odd numbers, i.e., 3, 5, 7, the starting player moves to the left-hand side of the court.

Player Positioning for Singles Pickleball

Generally, the rules for singles Pickleball games are the same as for doubles games, with two exceptions:

- Players only get one serve each.

- Because there is no first and second server, the score only has two digits.

The match begins with a serve from the even side, just like in doubles. The server moves to the left side if the serve is a one. The server holds the serve until a fault is committed or an opponent wins the rally. Serves must always be played crosscourt. A side-out is called should either happen, and the serve goes to the opponent.

Positioning of the server and receiver is crucial in both singles and doubles matches. Regardless of the score, servers and receivers must always stand on their respective sides of the court:

- **Even Score:** If the score is even, the serve must come from the right side of the server's court and be delivered to the receiver's right side of the opponent's court. This is known as serving crosscourt.

- **Odd Score:** If odd numbers are the only points within the score, the server switches to the left and serves across the court to the left of the receiver.

A server commits a fault if they are in the wrong place and lose the rally as a result. A fault can be made between the time the ball and racquet make contact and the subsequent serve if the referee or another player calls one.

- No one receives a point, and the server loses the serve if a fault is called before the following server serves. Regardless of the nature of the error and the positions of the players, the server nevertheless retains the points that were previously won.

- The point stands if the fault is not called until after the next serve.

- The result will stand if the fault is called when the match is on its final point. The exception to this is if the scoresheet hasn't yet been returned to the officials.

Introduction to Stacking

As you've just learned, player positioning is important in Pickleball, especially where the scores are concerned. To recap:

- If servers and receivers are not in the proper positions, they will make a mistake and lose the rally.

- Between the serve and the following serve, a player or the referee may declare a fault.

- The team serving loses the point if a fault is called before they play the serve, but they maintain the points they have already gained.

- If the next server has started when the fault is called, the team that committed it retains its point.

- If called on the last point of the game, the result is retained unless called before the scoresheet is handed to the officials.

However, while positioning is important, doubles games offer an advanced strategy to manipulate players' positions on the court. It is known as stacking and can help each team player remain on the same side of the court right through the game. In simple terms, players can stay exactly where they are. Some rules allow this strategy to be used:

- Provided the serving player is on the correct side, their partner can be anywhere on their side of the court, including on the court and off it.

- In the same way, provided the receiving player is standing on the correct side, their partner may also be positioned anywhere on their side of the court.

- Once the serve has happened, the serving team can change sides while the rally is ongoing. However, they should return to their original positions when the rally is over. Those positions are determined by where they started the game and the scores.

After returning the serve, the receiving team is allowed to swap sides while the rally is ongoing. When the rally is finished, they should go back to their original positions, determined by where they started the game and the score. Players tend to use stacking in the following scenarios:

- In a team, one of you plays right-handed, and the other plays left-handed. Stacking keeps both forehands to the court center.

- In a team where one player has a much stronger fore or backhand than the other, using stacking keeps the strongest hand near the court center, regardless of whether it is fore or backhand.

- If one player is stronger, that player might be stacked to ensure the player whose forehand is stronger is towards the center of the court. This means staying on the right-hand side.

- When the two players on the team are facing a specific opponent and have a string match-up.

Introduction to Rally Scoring

Rally scoring is different from traditional scoring. Only the serving team can score a point in traditional scoring, while rally scoring allows the serving or receiving team to score. This makes a game more dynamic because every rally means an opportunity for scoring points.

Players can use rally scoring in several ways, and we'll concentrate on Major League Events to give you an overview:

- Determining who plays at which end of the court can be ascertained by any method deemed fair to both sides. The same is also used to determine who serves first. Methods considered fair are coin flips and games like rock, paper, scissors.

- You must decide between you and your partner which side of the court you will play on. Each player stays on those sides while the entire game is played. However, players may change sides when an end change or a time-out occurs.

- The serving team begins the match by delivering a crosscourt serve from their even side to the opponent's even side.

- If the serving team wins the rally, they keep the serve and receive a point. The player on the left side of the court then plays the serve. Don't forget both players stay on their original sides. The serve continues to switch between members of the serving team until the opposition prevails in the rally.

- When the serving team loses the rally, the receiving team scores a point and receives the serve. Because there isn't a second server, the score only contains two numbers.

- The two numbers in the score correspond to the serving and receiving teams' scores. Which player serves depends on the score of the serving team; if the score is even, the player on the right serves, and if the score is odd, the player on the left serves. Assuming that the receiving team won the rally and the score is at 2-2. They win the point and serve, bringing the score to 3-2. In that case, the player to the left will take the next serve.

- When one team gets to 11 points, the teams swap ends of the court.

- The first team in a Major League game to accumulate 21 games, but only if they prevailed by at least two points. But after 20 points, you can only win points by serving. The other team can only score when they serve after stopping at 18 points when one team reaches 20.

Calling the Score in Pickleball

All players are prepared to play, and the server and receiver are in the proper positions, according to the score that is being announced. The score can still be called, and play will begin even if a server or receiver tries to purposefully stall the start and fails to take position.

When they are not ready to play, athletes should let other players know. This teaches the players that they shouldn't announce the score or smash a hard serve over the net before the recipient is prepared. There are two ways for players to let others know they're not ready:

1. Hold their Pickleball racquet over their head.

2. Turn around, facing away from the net; their back should face the net and the opposing team.

Once the scores have been called, players cannot continue to utilize these signals since they will be disregarded. Additionally, they shouldn't use these signals to try to stall the game.

If the server has trouble being heard, they can ask their teammates to announce the score. The individual who announces the score first, however, must do so for the duration of the game.

Calling the Wrong Score

Sometimes, the server or referee may call the wrong score. In such a case, play may be stopped by any player who can then ask for the score to be called again, this time correctly. The correct score must be called before the third shot of a rally is hit.

If a player stops the game to get the right score after the third shot, it is considered a fault. In this case, they lose the rally, and the serve goes to the other team. So, be aware that play can only be stopped legally before the third shot in case of an incorrect score. After that, it's not worth stopping play as the caller will lose the point and, possibly, the game.

If the right score has been called but a player still stops playing, a fault has been committed. The player will lose the rally and the point is awarded to their opponents.

A player has to appeal to the referee or the other players and make a statement to indicate that the score is incorrect. For example, a player can say, "Referee, we have 6, not 5."

In all honesty, this rule is only really important in tournaments or professional games. If you are playing for fun, you'll find things more lighthearted and play usually continues. That said, you may get to the stage where you are playing in tournaments, and, as such, you should understand the correct rules.

Asking the Referee

It's normal for players to ask questions while playing but this is only really acceptable when playing for recreational purposes. If you are playing in a tournament, you can only ask the referee questions related to the score.

Either team can ask the referee certain questions before the serve is made:

- What is the score?

- Which team should be receiving or serving?

- Are we standing in the right place?

Regardless of who asks, the referee will request a timeout and answer any questions given before the serve. The game then starts after the score is announced. If the inquiries are made after the serve, the official will ignore them, and the game will continue. If a team keeps posing questions in an attempt to drag out the game, the referee may award that side a technical fault.

Chapter 8: Mastering Singles and Thriving in Doubles Play

So, here we are and you should now understand Pickleball, and have a good idea of how to play it. That means we need to start considering strategy. This is a key part of any sport, but when that sport is as unique as Pickleball, strategy is critical. Playing the game correctly and getting the most form it means learning strategies and how to use them.

The good news? Plenty of people are ready to give you their opinions and unique perspectives on the game, including recreational players and pro tournament players. Learn them, understand them, and use them to create your own perspective.

One area where you absolutely must learn strategy is the difference between playing a singles match and doubles. It should be crystal clear to you that playing on your own against one other person is totally different from playing with another person.

This chapter will look at strategies for singles matches, followed by doubles matches. It will tell you some of the best strategies and mindsets you should be employing, and while we do this, you'll also get a refresher on some of the basic rules. This way, you can learn whether singles or doubles play is right for you and start working out your strategies.

Singles

When you play a singles Pickleball match, it's a real battle of wits. It's you against your opponent, your might against theirs. Your brain is trying to one-up them. However, while only having one person on either side of the net comes with some advantages, it has a few disadvantages, too.

The upsides are simple: you get to play on the whole court without worrying about a partner, and you don't need to worry about communicating with someone else. You can get on and focus on playing a great game. However, that makes everything that happens on the court your sole responsibility. You need to be everywhere on that court at the same time, having to work out where you think the next shot will land. That makes it quite a bit harder than a doubles game, and if you play an opponent with their wits about them, your game could end up exhausting.

15. *In a singles game, you have to do two people's work. Source: https://upload.wikimedia.org/wikipedia/commons/6/66/The_Ros setti_Brothers_GWR_Longest_Pickleball_Rally.jpg*

You see, a singles Pickleball court is no smaller than a doubles court, leaving you having to do two people's work. That said, Pickleball courts are significantly smaller than badminton or tennis courts, so you already gain from not having such a huge area to police.

Let's look at some singles strategies you can use in your gaming.

Player Positions

Playing a singles game means having to be completely aware of your position on the Pickleball court. If you don't pay attention, you could miss returning the perfect shot that could be a winner. So, step one in any game is to be fully alert. You must be prepared to make a dash across the court in a split second. However, you must also make sure that your starting position on the court gives the best advantage possible.

The ideal starting position for players in singles games is to stand on the left or right side but as close to the center line as you can get. This will ensure you are as close as possible to any shot that comes over the net.

So, what about your depth? While staying close to the center, you should also position yourself as far back on the court as you can while trying to stay in the bottom third.

Why?

Well, first, you get way more visibility. When you stand near the net, you can see the whole court. Second, I'm pretty sure you know that running backward is not that easy! It's also difficult to hit a ball that lands behind you. So, stand towards the back of the court near the center. You can see the whole court, which means when the ball is hit over the net, you'll see it, and you'll see which direction it's going.

Serving

Where you are positioned is especially important when you are serving. While you must be standing on the correct side, make sure you are near the center line. You also need to ensure you don't become predictable in your serve – learn new ways and vary them every time. You want to serve as long and deep as possible without committing a fault or going out of bounds. That way, your opponent has to move a long way back on their side of the court. If they are right at the back, you have plenty of time to get up to your kitchen line and get as big a head start as you can.

This is a great strategy when you are serving because your opponent is immediately on the defensive, while you can go straight onto offense. Try to be in this position whenever you serve.

Returning the Serve

If you are the receiver, i.e., your opponent is serving, you may not be able to score, but you can force your opponent into committing faults – legally, of course – and that will lose them the serve, which then passes to you.

So, how do you do this?

By ensuring you return the serve in a way that makes things difficult for them. Again, vary your shots. Perhaps you could dink the first shot and then go for a ground shot on the second. By varying your shots, they are always on the back foot because they don't know what you will do yet. More experienced players will fake a move or shot and then do something completely different. That's something to learn when you've been playing for a while.

Also, hit as deep as you can on your return serve, preferably deep into the corners. These are not easy shots to return, and there is a good chance your opponent will miss, and that's what you want. It also means that your opponent will struggle to get the right stance to receive your shot unless they stick to the area behind the baseline. In this way, it's virtually impossible for them to do anything other than a moving shot.

Third-Shot Drop Dive

As the server, you get an additional advantage or the third shot. When you serve, your opponent returns it, giving you ball possession. At this point, players normally move nearer the net.

What you want to do here is aim the ball for the kitchen; that will make your opponent move forward, thus bringing the game up to the net. Make sure you get as much height on the ball as you can, as this will make your opponent struggle to hit it back. Master this skill, and every Pickleball game will include a successful volley and, potentially, a winning one.

Doubles

Doubles games are a whole different ballgame, pun completely intended!

Some things are far easier in doubles games than in singles. You don't need to worry about covering the whole court because your partner is responsible for half of it. That means you don't need to move too far to keep control of the ball, which, in turn, means you can keep your swings grounded, foregoing the moving shot, which is more unstable.

It also means having another player to rely on during gameplay.

That said, doubles games bring certain challenges not seen in singles games.

16. You have to communicate with your partner in a doubles game.
Source:
https://www.flickr.com/photos/martinvirtualtours/47108420782

First, you must make sure you don't step on any toes, literally in some cases! Next comes communication between you and your teammate. If you can't communicate effectively, neither you will know what the other is doing and your strategy will be next to useless. Part of this is down to how much you have played together. If you are regular partners, you'll have a good idea of how you both play and think. If you have never partnered with each other before, communication might not be so easy. Talk with your teammates before the match and make sure you each understand your playing styles. If you can't work together, you won't win the game.

The other disadvantage is that you don't have the court to yourself. If your opponent hits a shot you know you could have returned, but it goes in your team partner's side, it will be disappointing that you can't get it especially if they fail to return it effectively or, worse, miss it altogether.

That means having to learn to play as a team and ensuring your mindset is set that way. If your partner does manage to return the shot, be happy!

Let's look at some strategies you can use in doubles games.

Player Positioning

As discussed earlier, when you play a singles Pickleball match, you should position yourself as far back and as near to the center as possible. Doubles games are different. Your relationship with your partner determines your positioning. The best way is for the serving player to position themselves behind the baseline while the other player stays close to the kitchen boundary. That way, all ground is covered.

If your opponent slams a long shot back at you, the serving player is there to get it; if a shallow shot comes back, the other player has it covered. And if it goes midway, you've both got it covered, but communication etiquette dictates that you and your partner agree on who will go for such a shot.

Communicating with Your Teammate

Communication is critical in doubles play; without it, neither player on your team will know what the other is doing. There are a couple of things you can do.

First, you could devise codes between you, a bit like catchers and pitchers do in baseball. You can use these codes to talk to one another without your opponent's knowing what you are saying, incredibly important in terms of strategy. For example, the player who isn't serving may want to tell the server what kind of serve would be best, and this could be done with a cough, a hand movement, or something similar. Nonverbal signals are an excellent form of communication, provided both of you fully understand the signals.

You could also come up with a few "what-if" scenarios between you ahead of the match. Decide ahead of time how you will manage certain scenarios that could come up during the game.

Communication is key to Pickleball, be it while playing or before the game. It is also the only way for you both to play together as teammates and increase your chances of winning.

Move Together

When you have served, you and your partner should coordinate your movements. This is sometimes called "string strategy," and it means imagining a string tethering you to one another, one that cannot be severed. When one of you moves left, the other goes with them. If they go backward, so do you. This synchronizes you and helps eliminate the risk of many common pitfalls.

Hit to the Middle

In a doubles game, you must keep one thing in mind. You aren't just playing a defensive game. You must also be on the offense. That means finding good ways to strengthen your advantage by weakening your opponent.

Aiming for center court is perhaps the best strategy you can use. This causes confusion in your opponents as to who will return the ball, especially if they are not communicating effectively with one another. You expose a weakness in their team, and, if nothing else, you slow down their reaction times. This leaves space and time for them to commit blunders, which gives you a great advantage.

No matter whether you are playing singles or doubles Pickleball, the most important things to remember are positioning and communication. Get these right, and you have a winning combination!

Chapter 9: Common Mistakes and How to Avoid Them

Mistakes – the bane of any Pickleball player's life, but everyone makes them. Sometimes, you'll make mistakes without knowing why or how to deal with them. This is especially true of newbie players, and it isn't always easy to find the answer – this is a relatively new sport, after all. This chapter is dedicated to looking at some of the more common mistakes made by beginner Pickleball players and how to deal with them.

Before delving into these, something should be made clear. All Pickleball players have made these mistakes, just like even the most experienced players had to start at the beginning. So please don't beat yourself up when you make one. Learn from your mistakes and let them help you improve.

Not Moving from No Man's Land

There are two places a player should stand during a point, and these are the kitchen line and the baseline. Most of the time, you don't need to be anywhere else on the court, but if you are outside these two places, you are in what is known as No Man's Land.

A rookie mistake, one made by most beginners, is to stay there. It means you are hanging around between the kitchen and the baseline, and you really don't want to be there.

Why?

Well, first of all, when you stay there, your opponent can easily hit their shots at your feet, and these are notoriously difficult shots to return at the best of times. Add in the fact that you'll likely be running as well, and you put yourself in a near-impossible situation to get out of. Should you make contact with the ball, all you'll achieve is hitting it into the net or sending it flying. In the latter case, your opponent has the perfect return shot.

When you linger in no man's land, you run the chance of being hit with the crosscourt dink, one of the hardest shots to return. You could easily knock these back if you were standing at the kitchen line, but not in no man's land.

Nevertheless, if you remain in the kitchen line, your adversary may throw a shot in your direction. Most players don't do this because they know the risk involved. Lob shots can easily be smashed back by an alert, fast player, or they may even go out of bounds. Crosscourt dinks are a much safer bet.

Thus, the first rule to improve your game is to get to the kitchen line after the serve and return serve are done.

Hitting to Your Opponent's Forehand

One of the most basic concepts you should learn in Pickleball is this. Let your opponents make the mistakes. In fact, let them do as much of the work as possible and reap the rewards! That's how many players win their games. What you shouldn't do is give your opponent an easy ride. That means you must avoid hitting the ball to their forehand. You should be focusing on their backhand, and there's a good reason for that.

It doesn't matter how skillful a player may be. Most player's backhand is much weaker than their forehand. While some players won't fall in with this, you will find it with most, especially in recreational games. So, you need to use that against them. Think about it this way: if your backhand is much weaker, do you want your opponent hitting a ball to it? No. Not only will it force you out of position, but it will also be much harder for you to hit with any real power. Your forehand, of course, because you have a much better chance of returning it. If they hit to your backhand, you'll struggle, and that's what you want your opponent to do!

Some shots are more important than others for this strategy:

- Serve
- Third shot drop
- Crosscourt dink

The crosscourt dink is especially important.

Imagine you are playing a doubles match and controlling the court's left side. When you dink crosscourt, you go for your right. We could also assume that your opponent is right-handed. In that case, you really should avoid hitting your dink to their forehand.

Why?

You are much closer to the net, and you need a bigger angle for a crosscourt dink so that the ball skims low over the net. Hit it too high, and you'll just get it smashed back at you.

Moving Past the Baseline When Serving

Another mistake you rarely see in tournaments is a player serving the ball and immediately moving past the baseline.

Why is this a mistake?

The double bounce rule is one which prevents you from volleying on the return serve.

Think about serving the ball. Your opponent slams the ball back after returning your serve as you move forward across the baseline. Since you have advanced, you are unlikely to catch the deep ball. It is considered a fault if you strike it before it bounces.

Remain in place. Once you have served, stay put behind the baseline and wait. This is more so if you are playing experienced opponents, as they will likely lob a deep shot back. Your partner should do the same on their serve, too.

Hitting Fancy Spin Shots

There's nothing wrong with hitting a fancy spin shot, per se, but it will rarely end well. Yes, you can use them, but don't overdo it, or it will lead to mistakes.

This is especially true if your opponents are experienced; they've been there and understand those shots well. They know how to get around them or use them against you.

The biggest problem with spin shots, fancy or otherwise, is that pulling them off requires accuracy and skill. If you are a beginner player, avoid using them. Many pro players won't even use them because the potential for disaster is too great.

Winning a game of Pickleball is about persistence, strategy, and consistency, not getting fancy with your shots in a bid to outwit your opponents. Used in the right way, a spin shot can work, but not when you consistently try to get fancy with them and use them all the time.

Playing with the Wrong Racquet

The Pickleball racquet is one of the most important pieces of equipment. As in any sport, the racquet must be right for you, or you won't play a good game. That said, the one thing that must be made clear is that you shouldn't blame your mistakes on your racquet. There's likely nothing wrong with it, and the racquet has little to do with playing with technique and skill.

That said, your racquet must suit you. Otherwise, you really won't play very well. Some signs that your racquet isn't right are:

- You get serious problems in your arms, elbows, and/or wrists.
- The racquet is too heavy and slows you down.
- It's not heavy enough to allow power behind your shots.

The first of those points is one of the most critical. You must stop using your racquet immediately if you feel fatigue or pain in your wrists, elbows, or arms. Find a new one that suits you better. Just remember that what you might find heavy won't be heavy to another player, so be careful when choosing your racquet. Try a few and see what weight racquet works best for you.

Only Using a Power Game

While one of the most fun parts of the game is smashing the ball back as hard as you can, you don't need to hit every shot that way, especially when playing pro games.

Why?

For two reasons.

First, risk or reward, something that seems to rule a large proportion of the human race! One of the most unpredictable types of shots is the power shot, and, to be honest, they aren't the prettiest to watch, either. This is even more the case when used on third-shot drives. Adding variation is the only real way to knock your opponent off their balance. Throwing a power shot in now and then is the best way. These are fast and random, and unless you constantly use them, your opponent won't be expecting them. A power shot can also go out to the baseline or hit the net, which is no advantage to you.

Second, these shots don't really work when you are playing experienced Pickleball players. They've seen just about everything you could possibly hit their way, especially if you are a beginner. They've blocked so many of these shots that they are no longer surprised by them. An experienced player will merely block a power shot into your kitchen zone, especially if you use it on a third-shot drive. And you know what? There's not a darn thing you can do about it!

Power shots may be useful, but they have their place. Stop trying to use them all the time and stick to using them on occasion to achieve an advantage or win a point.

Forehand Player Not Taking Center-Court Shots

This isn't just a rookie mistake; it also happens with more experienced players, especially when communication between players isn't effective.

An unspoken rule in doubles Pickleball is that the person with the strongest forehand takes the shots that head up the center. Obviously, that comes down to whether they are left-handed or right-handed.

Let's imagine a scenario. You and your partner are both right-handed, and you are positioned on the left of the court. In that case, with the dominant forehand, it's your responsibility to take all the shots that go up the center, even the smash shots.

Why?

It's simply because the left player can use their strong forehand, which is much easier than the backhand.

Not Sprinting to the Kitchen

Pickleball is mostly played in the kitchen zone, not the center of the court and not the baseline, but the kitchen.

That means getting there quickly is critical to success. In much the same way as staying in no man's land for too long, staying away from the kitchen makes you a good target for the opponent to smash a ball to – one you likely cannot hit back.

If you are not terribly mobile and cannot sprint, just try to get there as quickly as possible. If you are en-route to the kitchen and the ball comes towards you. Stop. Focus on returning it before continuing. Running and hitting a ball back simultaneously is quite difficult. Try it, and you'll probably mishit the ball and give your opponent an easy shot.

Poaching When You Don't Need to

Do you know what poaching is? Let's explain it quickly before looking at the mistake.

Poaching is when you steal a shot from your partner. Think about it. Let's say you are playing doubles, and a dinking rally is going on. You go to hit the ball, and your teammate dives in and hits it for you. Now, wouldn't that irritate you?

Poaching is a strategy of sorts but more of an advanced one. Take some time to watch pro games – live or find some videos online. You'll likely see "stacking" in most games. Cast your mind back, and you'll remember I told you this meant having a player on each side of the court.

During a mixed doubles game, you will find the female player plays on the right-hand side while the male player stays left. When the forehand smash shots come in, they are usually hit by the male player, even though they head towards the female. This is how to poach effectively.

However, there is no benefit to ineffective poaching. Poaching a shot means having to move over to your partner's side of the court or near it, and that results in a big gap on the court. Your opponent will aim for that gap and likely win the point. The only time you should poach is when there is no way for your opponent to hit it and recover it.

You also shouldn't poach your partner's shots without discussing it with them beforehand. Communicate, talk to your partner, and get their agreement.

Crosscourt Dinking Battles against Better Players

Crosscourt dinking is fun, as are dinking battles at times. They test your playing skills and your stamina and reflexes but they are not appropriate all the time. It's a risky business to go up against a more experienced player, especially if you haven't been playing long.

On the Pickleball court, avoiding annihilation is actually fairly simple. Count the dinks if you find yourself in a crosscourt dink rally with an expert player. Go for a bailout when your opponent returns your third dink. Send the ball to the player's partner rather than dinking it back to them. You not only lower your chance of losing but the momentum and direction are also altered.

One more thing: if your teammate is a better dinker, bring them into play using this strategy.

Trying to Hit a Shot You Can't Get

Many players struggle with this, even pro players. Every player wants a fun and exciting game, not one full of predictable, boring gameplay. So, why not aim for an impossible shot you know you can't hit?

That said, you shouldn't do this if you are trying to improve. Don't try to hit shots you know you can't hit. It will end in disaster, that's a fact. At best, you'll miss it and, at worst, it'll go out of bounds so far you'll be lucky to find the ball again!

That doesn't mean that you shouldn't hit important shots. It means you don't try to hit shots you absolutely know you have no chance of succeeding at.

Trying to Smash a Low Ball

Another highly frequent error is this one. Do you ever watch a game and question why a player on the kitchen line manages to smash a ball into the net?

Usually, this occurs when a player shoots a third shot that drops slightly high but doesn't gain enough height. The ball enters a space where volleying ought to be simple, but they are unsure if they will be able to smash the ball back. The majority of amateurs who attempt to slam the ball down from the kitchen zone only succeed in hitting it into the goal.

Getting around this is easy.

Don't smash the ball back. Shift your racquet in the same direction you want the ball going. Should you try to hit an overhead smash, your racquet is facing the wrong way. It will face the ground, and that is where the ball will go. It won't go where you want it, to the other side of the court. The ball is way ahead of you, you won't be able to hit it at the top of its arc where you want to. Instead, you'll catch it at the end, and that's why it will hit the net.

Wherever you push your racquet, that's the direction you will send the ball. It may not have the power you want, but it will have accuracy.

Using a Hard Smash on Your Opponent's Power Shot

Did you ever play an opponent who smashed such a hard ball at you that you hit it out of bounds on the return? Pretty much every player has done it, even the pros. There is a simple answer to this. If a power shot comes your way, don't swing at it. These shots are hard and fast by design, and you don't need any more power to get it back over the net. Don't swing at them. Simply go for the block. Position your racquet so it's in the way of the ball, and the ball's power will take care of the rest.

Now, that doesn't mean this will be easy. It takes practice, and it's inherent in all players to want to hit the ball, not block it. Learn it well and get plenty of practice. It's sure to bring a real change to your game.

More importantly, you must understand that improving your game is not quick. It takes practice and determination, and while it is fun to play, it is also hard work. Practice, play, and learn from any mistakes you make. That way, you'll improve your game consistently.

Chapter 10: Tips from Pickleball Experts

As a beginner Pickleball player, do you find it enough to get the ball back across the net? The more you play, the more you will understand the rules and get a feel for the game. You'll be faster with better reactions, you won't make so many mistakes, and your skills will increase quickly.

But that all takes time.

One disturbing thing you might find is that you start to lose more as you get better. Why? Because you are playing better, more experienced Pickleball players. The only way to beat these players is to have the right strategy, a winning one, and you can only get that if you take note of the experts.

So, Let's look at what they have to say – some of it will seem familiar.

Talk, Talk, and Then Talk Some More

17. Talk to your partner to coordinate your strategy. Source: https://www.pexels.com/photo/happy-adult-sportspeople-standing-in-autumn-park-and-talking-7266726/

You don't see many singles Pickleball games as most are played as doubles matches, and to be fair, it's more challenging and fun. However, it does mean the team partners must talk to each other. You need to know who will take the first serve and who has the strongest forehand. Which one of you prefers to play backhand?

The only way to find all that is to communicate. Before you play, talk about your respective playing styles:

- Do you work your way up to the non-volley zone based on shots, or do you tend to belt to it?

- Do you prefer to play on the right of left side?

- Is your backhand string?

- How can your playing styles work together?

Your strategy should also showcase your strengths while minimizing any weaknesses you have. In other words, cover each other's backs.

For example, agree that when a shot goes straight up the middle, whoever hits it will shout, "Mine" first. This eliminates doubt and ensures the right person hits the ball.

Or when you score a point, celebrate by saying "Good job!" to your partner. Encourage each other when you've played a rally, regardless of whether you win. Be positive all the time. Encouragement and communication, be it verbal or nonverbal, is critical to ensuring you both play a good game.

Get to the Kitchen Line

Most points in any Pickleball rally are won by players near or on the kitchen line. That means getting up there as quickly as possible is important as, in that way, you can get into the best position.

The nearer you get to your opponent, the quicker your rallies will be. Always be ready. When you and your partner are at the line, your opponents will see a wall, which can work against them. It will put them on the defense, leaving you to go on the offense.

Your teammate should already be waiting at the line if the serve can be returned. Pressurize your opponents by moving the kitchen line when you return the serve to get your offensive game going.

That said, as I'm sure you have figured out by now, the kitchen line isn't always the safest place to be! You can expect much faster balls and the last thing you want is one of those hitting you in the face! Not only that but your racquet should be held up ready to hit the ball when it comes over.

You also need to remember not to enter the kitchen zone or stand on the line when you hit the ball. If you do, you incur a fault, and the point goes to your opponent.

Practice Dinking

Dinking can help you warm up a the beginning of the game. It can also help you slow down the gameplay to give you time to set up your strategy.

Normally, you would dink near the kitchen line, hitting the ball in a low arc to the kitchen zone on your opponent's side. If you hit it right, the ball should bounce into their kitchen zone; this means your opponent must let it bounce before they go for it, as they can't get it any other way.

Always remember that the ball should stay near the net. This stops the ball from going high, which means your opponents won't get the chance to return it. Hitting dinks makes your opponent move, and they need to work to get that shot. Unlike the hard shots, the dink lacks power and doesn't require players to use their reflexes too much.

What you could do is dink crosscourt rather than straight across. This offers a couple of advantages:

- **Length:** hitting crosscourt gives you less chance of making an error because you have more space on the court.

- **Height:** The middle of the net is the lowest part; crosscourt dinks send the ball over the middle, allowing you to keep it lower. On the other hand, it also means you can hit the ball higher, dropping it into their kitchen zone.

Dinking crosscourt allows you to hit a softer but slightly higher ball. This allows it to get across the net but not so far across the court even the slowest player could hit it. It needs to go high enough to crop down into your opponent's kitchen, which means they can't hit it before it bounces. However, beginners will find this tough to grasp. Hitting a diagonal ball gives you more height – eight more inches, to be precise – and this makes success more likely. Get some well-played crosscourt dinks in, and you can force your opponent into moving, leaving the court open and the advantage yours.

Mix Up Your Shots

Unpredictability is a winning strategy, and you should use it as much as you can. Consistency in your shot types means your opponent will know where you will hit the ball and what type of shot to expect. That makes it easier for them to plan their shots and stop you from winning the point or even the game. Mix things up, not just the type of shot you use, but your pace, angle, and spin.

The following tips will help you:

- Change the height of your shots. Now and then, hit your opponent with a high lob.

- Use a mixture of soft and hard shots, but don't consistently alternate them.

- Switch between top and backspin.

- Use angles occasionally, but keep in mind that the middle is the safest place to be.

- Vary your pace.

If you want to win, don't let your opponent know what your strategy is; make them guess all the way through.

Don't Forget the Wind

If you play outdoors, keep the wind in mind, as a Pickleball ball is light and will easily be taken by a gust. That said, you should be using the right ball, as there are specific ones for indoor and outdoor play. Outdoor balls have much smaller holes, which helps keep them steady on windy days.

When you are warming up, note the velocity and direction of the wind – your gameplay will need to be adjusted to take them into account. One tip you should play by is this. Allow the wind to put you in position. If you can feel the wind against your chest, move backward.

A ball will come at you fast when it comes in on the wind. It is liable to land very deep, if not behind the baseline. If you feel the wind on your back, move forward. It means your opponent is hitting it into the wind, and their balls won't go so far. If it blows crossways, try to aim toward the middle; that way, the ball can move with the wind but still land within bounds.

Target Your Opponent's Backhand

When you improve your game and learn to place your shots better, you can begin to target their backhand, especially by aiming low at their feet. Most players are stronger on their forehand and will position them to take advantage of it. By targeting their backhand, you force them to turn so they can hit the ball, putting themselves out of position and giving you the advantage so make it count on the return.

Your opponents will get confused when you aim the ball toward the center but at one of their backhands. Neither of them will be able to hit the ball properly, if at all. This is best used for singles matches, as they give you better opportunities for targeting your opponent's backhand.

Work on Your Footwork

Correct footwork is critical in Pickleball. If you are slopping about all over the court, you will struggle to hit the shots properly. Standing still and stretching your racquet toward the ball won't help, either.

When your footwork is right, you can move easily around the court, getting into the right position. Use the following drills to help you:

- Practice at home. Hit balls against a wall, keeping your focus on moving your feet. This teaches you how to move with the ball, allowing you to follow its direction instead of stretching your racquet out to hit it.

- You must be parallel, as this solidifies your center of balance when hitting the ball.

- Try not to land on your heels. Your heels aren't as flexible as the balls of your feet, and they don't align with your center of gravity. Landing on your heels will slow you down.

- Position your feet no wider than shoulder-width apart. If they're any wider, you won't be able to move properly.

Mastering footwork is a great advantage and can help you win.

Get to Grips with the Third Shot Drop

The third shot drop is an incredibly important shot to learn. The shots go like this:

1. Serve

2. Return Serve

3. Third Shot

The serving team gets the third shot, which you need to learn to hit as a drop shot. Drop shots let you move quickly to the kitchen line. Don't forget, the receiving team already has a player at the line when the rally begins. As soon as the serve is returned, the other player goes to the line, and that's where you need to be, too.

The third shot drop is a lot softer and, hit correctly, will go over the net, dropping into the kitchen one on the other side. The time it takes for the ball to bounce before being struck by your opponent allows you to get to your non-volley line.

Follow these tips to help you:

- This is called the third shot drop for a reason; it happens on the third shot of the game. Serve the ball, wait for it to be returned, and drop it into the kitchen zone.

- Get your racquet underneath the ball to lift it. You can use your knees to help you. This ensures the ball goes up and forward but not fast, and it will drop on the other side of the net into their kitchen zone.

- Be aware of your angles. If your hit is too deep, your opponents will have the chance to smash it back.

- Timing is critical. The ball needs to be low when you hit it. You won't get the pace or arc you need if it is too high, and your opponent can strike the ball back at you.

- Most importantly, once you hit the third shot drop, move straight up to the kitchen line.

Critically, make sure your opponents are on the defensive, giving you the time you need to reach the net.

Use Your Partner

You play as a team and need each other to win, so don't ignore each other. Communicate all the time. If your partner hits well, give them space to play, but if they struggle, think about poaching to help out.

Move in tandem and coordinate because, in that way, you won't leave any gaps where your opponent can get through and win a point. There's an old saying that is very true in this case – "United we stand, divided we fall." If you can't play with your teammate, you cannot win the game.

Always Get Your Serves In

When you watch a tennis match, you see fast-paced hard serves that win points, but that doesn't mean you can bring that kind of play to Pickleball. The serve is the only way to bring the ball into the game in Pickleball, so getting your serve in is important for two reasons:

1. You get one serve, and if you don't get it in, you don't get another go.

2. Only the serving team can score points.

Practice the serves regularly. Flip between average and fast serves, high and low arcs, and aiming at different areas of the court. However, remember that while variety is great, the most important thing is to get the serve in.

Let's say you are playing second serve and feel the urge to hit the ball with plenty of spin or angle. If you do, you'll only pass the ball to your opponent, and they get the chance to score.

Make sure you get the ball into the game and play the rally. That's the only way to determine who wins and loses the game.

Push Your Opponents Back

One of the most important things to do in Pickleball is make your way to the kitchen line as fast as you can. However, it is also important to force your opponents to go back to their baseline and then keep them there. The longer they are there, the more difficult the shots they have to hit, and this might not be comfortable for them.

There are a few ways you can do this:

- When you serve, hit them deep and near the baseline.

- When returning a serve, hit as deep as possible with an arc. Your opponent will not be able to hit the ball until it bounces, which will give you time to set up your offense. Try to aim for your opponent's feet at the furthest point on the court.

- Throw a fast serve in occasionally and, if possible, add a little spin. This knocks your opponents off-guard. However, do practice this – a lot – before you take it to a match; if it goes wrong, it won't be to your advantage.

Forcing your opponents' back and keeping them there gives you a strong advantage in a Pickleball game.

Play Strategic Shots

Pickleball isn't just a game of skill; strategy is critical to success. The right strategy can even knock an experienced player off their game, and one of the most important keys to building your strategy is court awareness.

Beginner players are likely to be highly focused on actually making contact with the ball. However, the more improvement they make, the more strategic they must learn to be, and more aware of what is going on around them in a rally. That means knowing how and when to change strategy based on what their opponent is doing. Let's say your opponent has moved to the net, so you decide to hit a drop shot and not a drive-through shot. Or if your opponent has had to go back to their baseline, you could drive a drop shot into the kitchen zone. If your opponent constantly slams shots at you, the ability to play a good soft game and block their shots will stand you in great stead.

The one thing you must do is learn where your opponent's weak points are; then, you can use them to your advantage. If it's possible to force your opponent over to the left of the court, you have an open court to place your shot into. The important thing is not to let your adrenaline get the better of you. Never rush your shots, as unintentional mishits are a real possibility.

Are You Playing Offense or Defense?

You can play a defensive or offensive game during a rally, and you can quickly switch between them. You might decide to start a rally on the offense, quickly switch to a defensive game, go back to offense, and so on.

The important thing is to know which you are playing. Otherwise, you cannot take advantage of the opportunities that might arise.

Let's say you are in control of your own kitchen line. Your opponent has moved to the middle of the court, which means you can play an offensive game. You go on the attack while they spend all their time in defense and attempting block shots.

Don't let your attack weaken. If your opponents do catch you out, you need to switch immediately to a defensive game. If you don't switch quickly enough, you could lose the point.

Serving Tips

These expert tips relate directly to serving:

- **Don't Go for a Hard Serve.** Accuracy is more important than power, so don't smash the ball as hard as you can. Try to aim toward the middle of your opponent's service box. This may cause them to make mistakes that you can use to your advantage.

- **Try a Little Spin.** Spins make your opponent have to work harder to get the ball back to you. Do practice your spins before you start using them in games, though, as they can backfire on you. And don't overdo your use of them.

Beginner's Tips

When you are new to anything, you should always be prepared to take advice and tips from others with more experience; Pickleball is no different.

- **Accept Feedback and Advice.** It will take a lot of consistent practice to get the game right, and you will make mistakes. Don't beat yourself up when you do. Watch videos, take lessons, and ask other players for feedback and advice. However, if you don't hear what you want to hear, don't get upset. The trick is to learn from your mistakes and practice where needed.

- **Keep the Ball in Play.** At least 75% of rallies are lost because of a daft mistake, so make sure placement and accuracy take center stage. Forget trying to be fancy and drive power shots, as they'll just get you into trouble.

- **Use the Continental Grip.** This allows you to control the ball better, and you'll find hitting angled, soft shots easier, meaning you can cause your opponent a little trouble. You can use this grip on the backhand and forehand easily without adjusting.

Tips for Intermediate Players

If you think you are good enough to move up a level, have a look at the tips below:

- **Master Dinks.** You absolutely must master these as they are the most effective shot in the game. It can force your opponent to move from their comfort zone and open up scoring opportunities for you.

- **Own the Kitchen Line.** Practice and train yourself to play close to the non-volley line. If you need to move backward to hit the ball, get back to the line quickly. This is where your point-scoring opportunities are at their best.

- **Hit Low Balls Slow and High Balls Hard.** Low balls should always be hit gently, but high shots from low positions frequently end up going high and out of bounds, striking the net, or being returned by the opposing team. The best use for a high ball is overhead slams, which should secure the ball for a point.

Chapter 11: Staying Safe and Injury-Free

The previous chapters have got all the fun of learning how to play Pickleball out of the way, so now it's time to discuss something incredibly important, and that's safety on the court. When the game gets exciting, safety tends to be pushed to the backburner, but it shouldn't be. Staying free of injury is the only way to truly enjoy your game.

Avoiding Common Pickleball Injuries

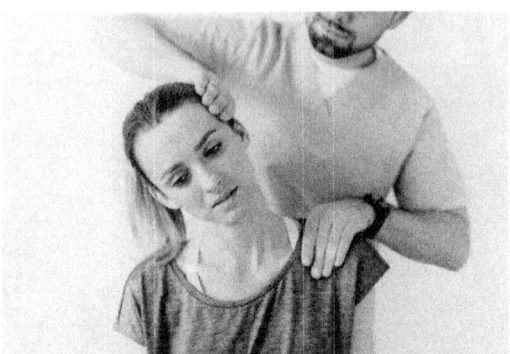

18. Common injuries among beginners include muscle strains. Source: https://www.pexels.com/photo/professional-massage-therapist-treating-a-female-patient-s-injured-neck-4506214/

Pickleball injuries are common among beginners, and these are the ones you will most likely get if you are not careful:

- Muscle strains

- Shoulder injuries

- Sprained ankles

- Tennis elbow

- Torn tendons/ligaments

Take the right precautions ahead of time and you can avoid most of these. Let's discuss those now.

- **Warming Up/Cooling Down:** Everyone should do this before and after every workout, and the same applies to playing sports. Warming up your body before you start playing helps prevent many injuries from happening. Do some stretches or go for a very light jog on the court, as it really does help. Cooling down will also help you stretch your muscles after exercise and can make recovery quicker. It also reduces sore muscles and fatigue. Deep breathing and static stretching are excellent ways to do this after a Pickleball game.

- **Maintain the Correct Playing Technique:** This doesn't just make your game better; it also reduces injury risks. When swinging your racquet, keep your wrist firm and steady. Play on your toes and bend your knees a little. One of the biggest causes of injury is not getting your techniques right, so consider taking professional lessons if you need to.

- **Using the Equipment Properly:** Make sure you are using the right equipment. Your racquet must be good quality and suit you and your playing style, or you risk stress injuries. The same goes for footwear; wear good quality sports shoes with great grip and support. And don't forget your glasses and other protective gear, especially when playing outdoors.

- **Court Safety:** Make sure you look at the court before the game begins. If anything is lying about that shouldn't be, get rid of it or it might cause an accident. Also, be aware of the boundaries so you don't fall or stumble.

- **Keep Fit:** Being physically fit helps prevent injuries. Do cardiovascular exercises regularly to keep your stamina up and strength training to build up your muscles and physical fitness. Don't leave out flexibility exercises. Yoga and stretching exercises are excellent as they increase your ability to recover in the event of an injury, and they keep you fit.

- **Listen to Your Body:** It knows when it is too tired to carry on or not fit enough, and it will tell you. If fatigue comes on, stop. Stop as soon as you feel pain, even a small pain, and have a doctor look at it. Pushing through your pain barrier is not something to be proud of; it will do you a lot of physical damage.

- **Stay Hydrated and Eat a Healthy Diet:** Water is one of the most important factors in anyone's life, not just sports people. Drinking plenty can help stop many injuries from occurring. Have a sports bottle handy and sip water throughout your game. Make sure you eat a decent diet, too. It should be highly nutritious, especially when you are playing professionally,

- **Don't Play with Pickleball Balls in Your Pockets:** This isn't tennis or cricket! You may think it's easier, and you would be surprised at how many newbie players do it, but the balls can injure you. If you fall over and land on one, it can injure your hips. Leave the balls on the bench where they belong.

- **Wear the Right Glasses:** That means not wearing your regular glasses or sunglasses. Always wear specific sports glasses. If necessary, you'll need to get them made up with your prescription. They should be made of a material that doesn't shatter and protects your eyes from the sun. Standard glasses will shatter if a ball hits them and can potentially cause a serious injury to your eye.

Returning to Play

If you have been injured, you must ensure you have recovered fully before returning to the Pickleball court. Start slowly, perhaps with a little light practice, before you start playing full games once more. Importantly, take note of what your doctor says!

Good Warmup Exercises:

Hamstring Stretch

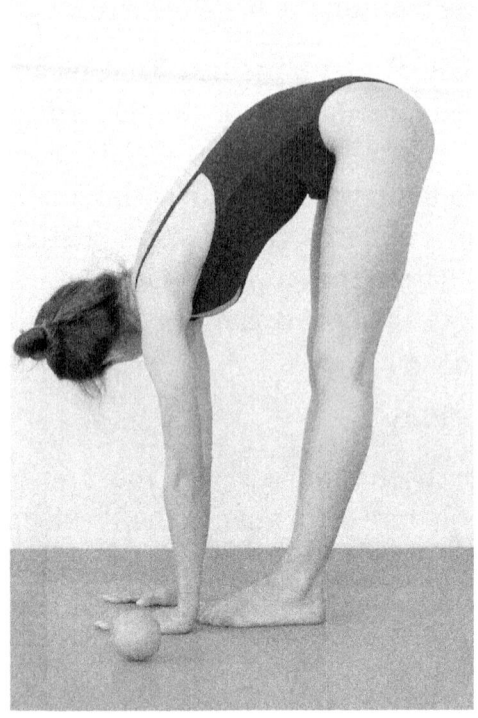

19. The hamstring stretch. Source: https://www.pexels.com/photo/person-woman-orange-hairstyle-8187592/

1. Stand up tall and straight with your feet placed hip-width apart.

2. Bend forward and reach for your toes.

3. Stay like this for 20 to 30 seconds, and then go back to the start.

4. Do these two or three times.

Quad Stretches

20. *Quad stretches.*
Sourcehttps://www.pexels.com/photo/concentrated-sportswoman-doing-quad-stretch-in-park-4426393/

1. Stand tall and straight with your feet together,

2. Bend one knee so you are standing on one leg. Your heel should be near your buttocks.

3. Grip the ankle with your hand, push your hips forward, and hold for 20 to 30 seconds, then release.

4. Go back to the beginning and do the same on the other leg.

5. Repeat a couple of times on each side.

Shoulder Stretches

21. *Shoulder stretches. Source: https://pixahive.com/photo/shoulder-stretch/*

1. Stand up tall and position your feet about shoulder-width apart.

2. Position your arm to the front of you, and use your right hand to hold it to your chest.

3. Stay like this for about 20 to 30 seconds, release, and do the same on the other side.

4. Do this exercise two or three times on each side.

Frequently Asked Questions

Let's finish with a few questions that get asked a lot about safety.

1. Is Playing Through My Pain the Right Thing to Do?

No, absolutely not. If you play through your pain, it can lead to injuries, so don't do it. If you feel pain, you must stop and go see your doctor.

2. I've Not Long Suffered a Small Injury; When Can I Start Playing Pickleball Again?

That is dependent on a couple of things, not least what the injury was and how bad it was. Plus, you should ask your doctor for advice before you begin playing again; they will tell you if you can or not.

3. How Do I Avoid Getting Tennis Elbow While Playing?

Quite simply, by warming up before you play and cooling down when you have finished. You should also exercise regularly and use the right techniques and equipment. If all this fails and you get persistent pain, you must stop playing and see your doctor for advice.

4. Do I Really Need to Wear Sports Shoes?

Absolutely. Wearing the right footwear is critical. Those designed for sports played on a court have the right support, are cushioned, and have the right grip to stop you from slipping and causing injuries.

As with everything, safety must come first. Whether this is your first or 101st game, the tips above can help you stay safe and stop you from getting injured.

Chapter 12: Getting Involved in the Pickleball Community

Pickleball isn't just a popular game, it is also a great community sport and keeps you fit. Here's why Pickleball should be a part of every community.

1. **It Encourages You to Move:** Pickleball is classed as low-impact and is one of the easiest sports to learn to play. Anyone can play it, no matter their age or ability. When you play Pickleball regularly, it keeps you fit. It improves your heart health, strengthens your muscles and lungs, and reduces the risks of some health conditions significantly, like obesity, diabetes, and heart disease.

2. **It Builds a Community:** Being such a social sport, Pickleball helps get people together in a sociable, friendly way. Whether you choose to play a family game or you want to meet other like-minded people, Pickleball is the way to do it, and it helps you build new bonds and deepen existing ones. This leads to better mental health, lower risk of stress, and a real sense of belonging.

22. Pickleball communities can help you meet like-minded people.
Source: https://unsplash.com/photos/toBavJYoM-
U?utm_source=unsplash&utm_medium=referral&utm_content=cr
editShareLink

3. **More Social Interaction:** Because you are meeting others, including new people, Pickleball offers a way of making new friends and socializing with like-minded people. It helps you connect with others in the best possible way, whether for fun or a serious game.

4. **It Improves Your Mental Health:** There have been plenty of studies on this, all showing that Pickleball is great for reducing stress and making you feel a whole lot better about things. That's because it is a social, physical game that can make you happy, relaxed, and even fulfilled.

5. **It Supports Local Businesses:** Pickleball communities provide support for recreation centers, parks, sports stores, and other local businesses. When you promote it in your community, you help those businesses to thrive.

Pickleball isn't just a sport. It creates a tightly-knit community, bringing people together. The tips below are designed to help you join in with the Pickleball community:

Attend Events

Involvement in your community is as simple as attending local events. Many clubs hold events regularly, such as tournaments, open play, and clinics. These don't just let you play Pickleball. They also allow you to meet players and potentially make some new friends, not to mention picking up a few tips.

Join a League

Leagues are another great way of getting involved in the Pickleball community. They provide a competitive and organized environment for all skill levels, from complete newbies to pro players. Joining a league can give you access to valuable information and tips on improving, not to mention allowing you to meet other players. Attend regularly, and you'll soon start to recognize others and build up friendships with them.

Volunteer at a Tournament

Tournaments are important in the Pickleball community, and volunteering can be a big step towards getting yourself involved. You get to talk to players of all levels and from other regions, and you can play against them and socialize. Tournaments are reliant on volunteers, from those who monitor the court to keep score, and when you contribute your time and help, it helps the sport to grow and, once again, lets you meet new people.

Go to a Pickleball Clinic

Pickleball clinics are great ways to improve your game and meet other people. More often than not, pro players and coaches teach these clinics and usually focus on specific aspects of the game, such as dinking or serving. Combining social interaction with skill development provides a great opportunity for advancement and social growth in Pickleball.

Join a Meetup Group

These are a great way of meeting others and joining the community. They include all skill levels of players and offer social gatherings, open play, and many other activities. Groups are normally held regularly and you can meet other players and build up a relationship with them. You can find details of your local meetups online.

When you get involved in your community, you get to enjoy a great new sport while socializing and making new friends who share your passions and interests. You can also get many tips, learn new strategies and techniques, and build lasting relationships.

The trick is just to get out there, join in, and have fun.

Bonus Chapter: Fun Pickleball Facts

Pickleball is fast becoming popular, not just nationally but internationally, too. Here are some fun facts about the sport to end this book.

20 Fun Facts

1. Among players and fans, players are often called "picklers."

2. Pickleball is suitable for all ages, but only about 35% of players are younger than 60.

3. More than 2,000 registered ambassadors are teaching and promoting Pickleball across the USA.

4. Although female and male players are required to adhere to the same regulations, they are only permitted to compete against one another in mixed doubles games.

5. Males make up about 70% of all players.

6. Many people start playing for the social aspect.

7. You can play Pickleball outdoors and indoors.

8. Naples, Florida, is the world Pickleball capital, hosting the US Pickleball Championships annually.

9. Pickleballs are plastic.

10. Pickleball is the lowest-impact racquet sport.

11. Pickleball serves must be underhand.

12. The 7 ft. court area close to the net is called the kitchen.

13. Picklers cannot hit the ball in the air from the kitchen zone.

14. The most commonly used Pickleball balls are the Onix Fuse, Penn 40, and Durafast 40.

15. There is even a dedicated Pickleball TV channel for people to pick up updates.

16. Pickleball racquets are available in a wide range of sizes, weights, forms, and core materials.

17. The USA Pickleball Association (USAPA) creates a Pickleball community through many different programs.

18. Tournaments may be singles or doubles.

19. A Pickleball court must be 20 x 44 feet.

20. The Pickleball net is 34 inches high.

20 Fun Facts about Pickleball's Origins

1. Pickleball was invented in 1965 by three Washington men to entertain their kids.

2. Bill Bell, Joel Pritchard, and Barney McCallum came up with Pickleball because they couldn't locate a shuttlecock to play badminton.

3. The equipment originated from things the inventors had lying around their homes, but it evolved yearly.

4. The Pickleball rules were adapted from those of badminton, table tennis, and tennis.

5. The first official court was built in 1967 in the USA.

6. The first Pickleball competition took place in Washington in 1976.

7. Some believe the game's name came from the term "pickle boat."

8. Others believe the game was named after Pickles, a cocker spaniel owned by Joel Pritchard. However, the dog only appeared in family pictures 2 years after the game was invented.

9. Another common belief is that Joel Pritchard's wife named the game because of the Pickle Boat.

10. A whiffle ball was used in early games.

11. The three investors designed oversized paddles to play the game.

12. The USAPA was established in 2005 to promote Pickleball.

13. The IFP (International Federation of Pickleball) was established in 2015.

14. In 2015, the very first US Open took place.

15. A book called "Other Racquet Sports" was the first to mention Pickleball in 1978.

16. Jennifer Lucore and Beverly Youngren, two former USAPA members, wrote the first history book on the sport, which was published in 2018.

17. Barney McCallum was 93 when he died in 2019.

18. The Professional Pickleball Registry (PPR) was created in 2018.

19. The USAPA name changed to USA Pickleball in 2020.

20. These days, thousands of clubs and sports parks allow Pickleball to be played for free.

20 Professional Pickleball Facts

1. The IFP constantly seeks recognition to get Pickleball accepted as an Olympic sport.

2. Players from all over the world take part in international Pickleball tournaments, including those from the USA, UK, France, Spain, India, and Canada.

3. Oregon, Washington, and California have more professional players than anywhere else.

4. The IPTPA (International Pickleball Teaching Professional Association) is available for those who want to rise to the elite player level.

5. Most professional players played another racquet sport before playing Pickleball.

6. Many injured or retired tennis players take up Professional Pickleball because it is a low-impact sport.

7. You can only score points in traditional Pickleball when you serve.

8. Even people who have never played another sport or who do little exercise can become pro players.

9. Pickleball demands less physical fitness than other sports.

10. The USAPA provides Pickleball balls and regulates them.

11. Official balls must have between 26 and 40 holes.

12. Pickleball is a way for pro players to be great athletes without risk to their bodies.

13. The biggest meetup was in 2018 in California, when more than 2200 players attended the national championships.

14. More than 17 hours of live Pickleball matches were streamed by the Margaritaville USA Pickleball National Championships.

15. Typically, pro players dress in shorts or sweatpants and wear polos or t-shirts.

16. Outdoor balls have small holes but have many of them.

17. Indoor balls have fewer holes, but they are larger.

18. Different competitions may allow colored balls.

19. Some venues turn badminton courts into Pickleball courts for tournament purposes.

20. The Pickleball Hall of Fame was established in 2017, so pro players could be properly recognized.

---

15 Weird Pickleball Facts

1. Pickleball doesn't have anything to do with pickles.

---

2. The game has no official dress code or uniform.

3. A feature called Places2Play was created by the USAPA to allow people to find out where they can practice.

4. The US Open is attended by over a hundred thousand spectators annually.

5. Pickleball offers everyone health benefits, especially middle-aged and older players.

6. Doctors recommend that people with Parkinson's disease play Pickleball.

7. Pickleball is great for exercising the mind.

8. In Pickleball terms, a player who wins has "pickled" the game.

9. Others say that the losers are "pickled."

10. Some players say that when they compete, they get a "Pickleball high."

11. Pickleball can improve your hand-eye coordination.

12. The USAPA designed a manual in 2017 about constructing and maintaining Pickleball courts.

13. Pickleball is popular in retirement communities.

14. A Pickleball ball travels at a third of the speed of a tennis ball; this is due to the holes.

15. Some people claim they are addicted!

18 Surprising Pickleball Facts

1. There were over 3 million players in the USA in 2019 but now, there are well over 6 million.

2. Statistics tell us that Pickleball is growing faster in the USA than most sports.

3. Schools worldwide teach Pickleball during gym classes, including elementary, middle, and high schools.

4. The USA is home to over 30,000 outdoor and indoor courts.

5. The youngest registered player is 4, and the oldest is 94.

6. Playing Pickleball for half an hour can help a 250-pound person burn up to 250 calories.

7. The rules were adapted to ensure Pickleball was inclusive.

8. The rules allow wheelchair players and standing players to compete against one another.

9. The USAPA membership has increased by more than a thousand percent since 2013.

10. Pickleball has helped many people build their self-esteem and beat depression.

11. It is one of the cheapest of all racquet sports.

12. You can burn off over 50% more calories playing Pickleball than you can by going for a walk for the same amount of time.

13. More people struggle with the kitchen rule than any other rule in the game.

14. You can join the USAPA for a yearly fee of just $35.

15. St. Jude's Children's Research Hospital became a USAPA national charitable partner in 2016.

16. When Pickleball is played socially, it helps release endorphins into the body.

17. Pickleball increases muscle activity.

18. There are more than 8,000 private and public locations in the USA where Pickleball can be played.

Conclusion

Thank you for reading this guide. I hope it was a fun read for you; it is, after all, a fun sport that is currently taking the world, especially the USA, by storm! I especially hope that you are now encouraged to join in.

Chapter 1 talked about where Pickleball originated, how it was named, and why it is such a great sport.

Chapter 2 walked you through getting started with Pickleball, including the equipment you need, how to choose the right racquet, and understanding the Pickleball court and ball.

In Chapter 3, you learned the important Pickleball rules, while Chapter 4 walked you through the best techniques for holding and using your racquet.

In Chapter 5, we talked about how you should navigate the Pickleball court, moving to the best positions for the best advantage. In Chapter 6, we discussed sportsmanship and talked about the right way to behave during a game, while in Chapter 7 we covered scoring strategies that will help you win, if not the game, then at least a point or two.

Chapter 8 looked at some strategies for playing in singles and doubles games, and in Chapter 9, you learned about common mistakes that you really should avoid.

Chapter 10 provided tips from expert players and strategies to help you improve, while Chapter 11 discussed ways to stay safe on the court and avoid injuries. Finally, chapter 12 discussed joining the Pickleball community and the benefits it brings.

Pickleball provides players with many benefits, whether it is played professionally or for fun. It doesn't just encourage you to get moving; it improves your mental health, encourages socialization, and helps build community spirit, making it one of the most social sports in the world today.

It doesn't matter whether you have played many times before or never, it is one of the most exciting games you will ever be involved in, and it will bring your community together.

If you enjoyed this guide, please leave a review for other potential readers, and, most of all, have fun!

References

10 Essential Pickleball Rules to Learn Before You Play. (n.d.). Paddletek Pickleball. https://www.paddletek.com/blogs/news/10-Pickleball-rules

13 Common Beginner Pickleball Mistakes And How To Fix Them. (2018, April 17). Pickleball Kitchen. https://Pickleballkitchen.com/13-common-beginner-Pickleball-mistakes-and-how-to-fix-them/

15 Pickleball tips to help you rack up more wins. (n.d.). Pickleheads. https://www.pickleheads.com/guides/Pickleball-tips

alan. (2022, October 21). Why Pickleball is Perfect for Any Age | Play Pickleball Denver CO. Achieve Sports. https://achievesports.com/why-Pickleball-is-perfect-for-any-age/

Hicks, S. (2012, January 26). Pickleball Rules of the Game: A Beginner's Guide. HowTheyPlay; HowTheyPlay. https://howtheyplay.com/individual-sports/Pickleball-rules-of-the-game-a-beginners-guide

How To Get Started In Pickleball: A Beginner's Guide. (2018, February 26). Pickleball Kitchen. https://Pickleballkitchen.com/get-started-Pickleball-beginners-guide/

https://www.facebook.com/primetimePickleball. (n.d.). Pickleball Hitting Techniques To Master Your Game - PrimeTime Pickleball. Https://PrimetimePickleball.com/. https://primetimePickleball.com/Pickleball-hitting-techniques/

Pickleball Ball Size, Weight & Material Guide | Net World Sports. (n.d.). Www.networldsports.co.uk. https://www.networldsports.co.uk/buyers-guides/Pickleball-ball-guide

Pickleball Etiquette: 19 Unspoken Rules for Newcomers. (n.d.). Paddletek Pickleball. https://www.paddletek.com/blogs/news/Pickleball-etiquette

Pickleball Scoring Rules – Learn How to Keep Score in Pickleball. (n.d.). Pickler. https://thepickler.com/blogs/Pickleball-blog/Pickleball-scoring-rules

Pickleball Serving Rules – Master the Start of Every Pickleball Rally. (n.d.). Pickler. https://thepickler.com/blogs/Pickleball-blog/Pickleball-serving-rules

Stay Injury-Free: Essential Safety Tips for Pickleball Players – Pickleball Pavillion. (n.d.). https://Pickleballpavillion.com/stay-injury-free-essential-safety-tips-for-Pickleball-players/

Stay Safe on the Court: Pickleball Players' Guide to Injury Prevention. (2023, February 21). Pickleball City Gifts. https://www.Pickleballcitygifts.com/blogs/blog-Pickleball-city-gifts/stay-safe-on-the-court-a-Pickleball-players-guide-to-injury-prevention

The History of Pickleball. (n.d.). Onix Pickleball. https://www.onixPickleball.com/blogs/learn-Pickleball/the-history-of-Pickleball

The Pickleball Community: How to Get Involved and Make New Friends - Sports Illustrated Pickleball News, Analysis and More. (n.d.). Sports Illustrated Pickleball News, Analysis and More.

https://Pickleball.si.com/guides/the-Pickleball-community-how-to-get-involved-and-make-new-friends

The Power of Pickleball: Building Strong Communities Through Sport. (n.d.). Www.linkedin.com. https://www.linkedin.com/pulse/power-Pickleball-building-strong-communities-through-sport-keca-ward-/

Unsicker, B. (2022, June 21). A Pickleball Paddle Buyer's Guide: How to Pick the Right Paddle for You. Pickleball Effect. https://Pickleballeffect.com/other/a-Pickleball-paddle-buyers-guide-how-to-pick-the-right-paddle-for-you/

What are the dimensions of a Pickleball court? (n.d.). Pickleheads. https://www.pickleheads.com/blog/dimensions-of-a-Pickleball-court

What Is Rally Scoring in Pickleball & How Does It Work? (2022, May 30). Pickler. https://thepickler.com/blogs/Pickleball-blog/Pickleball-rally-scoring

Printed in Great Britain
by Amazon

37486895R00086